Legends of Cades Cove and the Smokies Beyond

By Vic Weals

Published by

OLDEN PRESS
4403 Cypress Drive
Knoxville, Tennessee 37920

ISBN 0-9629156-2-9

Edited and Designed by
Vernon McKinney

Printed at
Quebecor World, Kingsport, Tennessee

Cover by Ken Canup

FOREWORD

I knew Vic Weals for half my life – 25 years. I met him in 1976 while he was writing his column, "Tennessee Travels," for The Knoxville Journal, as well as serving as a copy editor and wire editor, reviewing the Associated Press newswire for stories that would appear in the next day's editions of the newspaper.

I was a young copy clerk with a wife, two children, a GI bill to attend college and the dream of being a newspaperman. Vic helped me accomplish the latter, as he did so many other young journalists who toiled for the morning newspaper while trying to complete a degree or get to a larger newspaper somewhere else.

I would like to say that Vic was always patient in his teaching, but that would not be true. He loved to rattle our cages, make us think, challenge us in that thinking and make us prove our point. He usually did this with a smile, but a frown or raised bushy eyebrows over his glasses often put the exclamation mark on the lesson.

Vic retired in 1984 but continued the column until 1986. The signature logo for his column was a picture of Vic in a 1917 Model T Ford. He loved that logo but, alas, progress and redesign of the paper swept it away in later years to be replaced with a picture of Vic underscored by his name. He never liked it.

"Tennessee Travels," from which this anthology is drawn was his second column for The Journal. The first, "Home Folks," appeared six days a week from 1951-63. It was quite a task writing six columns a week, but Vic always found someone or something to write about. It was not until 1976 that "Tennessee Travels" appeared. It was published once a week, usually on Thursday.

As a copy editor, I often edited his column, wrote headlines and picture captions and designed the layout or the way it appeared in the newspaper. All of this was done with Vic's approval. If we disagreed on something, I would defer to him.

Vic spent years collecting these stories and photographs, convincing often reticent subjects to be interviewed and then recording them on a huge tape recorder that he lugged around East Tennessee.

He was among the first journalists in our area to use a tape recorder for interviews, an instrument that is now as common as a reporter's notebook.

Vic's first book, "Last Train to Elkmont," published in 1991, also explored the people of East Tennessee as well as the pioneer and lumber eras on the mountainous forks of Little River. It was an endeavor accomplished with the encouragement of his family.

In 1991 I interviewed him for an article about his book, and he said then he was working on a second one. Well, the "Legends of Cades Cove and the Smokies Beyond" is completed. And it is a delight. This collection of columns spans a number of years and offers a unique insight into Cades Cove and its people. It honors the common men and women who settled the primitive territory and made it their home until the National Park Service took the land in the 1930s for part of the Great SmokyMountains National Park.

These stories and others led to Vic being honored in 1984 by the East Tennessee Historical Society with its first History in the Media Award. The society noted Vic's attention to "telling the stories of individuals against the background of the times and places in which they lived."

A colleague, Robert Jones, neatly summarizes our friend Vic Weals: "He treated everyone with dignity, especially the hard-working men and women who worked outdoors in the fields, hills and mountains in an era that has almost faded away.

"He gathered oral history and photographs from hundreds of people, many of whom have no doubt passed on and would have taken their stories with them if not for Vic.

"His legacy will be the tremendous amount of local history he recorded for future generations to learn of the hardships and pleasures of life in the post-pioneer era of the Tennessee mountains."

His book is our pleasure.

– Thomas F. Chester
Deputy Managing Editor
The Knoxville News-Sentinel

Table of Contents

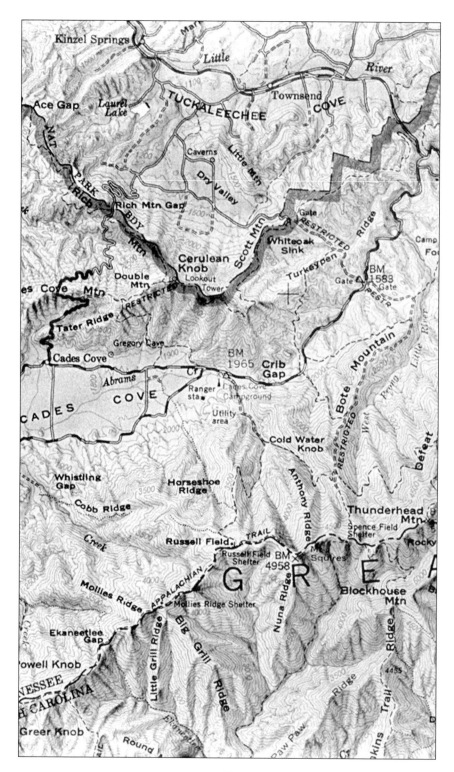

LIFE IN THE SMOKIES

1

Smokies bountiful to its people

Many of the people who lived in the Smokies a few years ago spoke of the entire main ridge and all of its peaks in the singular. From Davenport Gap on the east to Deals Gap on the west they thought of it all as "the Smoky Mountain."

John McCaulley and family and their Cades Cove neighbors were foraging 75 years ago and more along what they called the Bald Range, in and around the meadows of Gregory Bald and Parsons Bald.

To those who knew when and where to harvest it, the mountain was an abundant provider. Before his death in 1961 McCaulley recited some of the lore he had learned, from his first decade of life after 1880. "We had stock in the mountains all the time. We had hogs, calves and sheep.

"My daddy was a great mountain man. When we got the crop in (planted) in the spring of the year we'd take the calves and the hogs and everything and we'd take them to the mountain and stay a week with them, until they'd get settled down, get stationaried there.

"We'd squirrel hunt. Have a big time. Catch groundhogs and coons.

"I've spent half of my life on Smoky Mountain – laid out just everywhere night come on me. Didn't make no difference with me. Why I just laid down there and went to sleep – kindled me up a fire.

"Got up next mornin' and went on about my business.

"We ranged cattle there for years. I had a brother that stayed there in the herd cabin for three years, right on a straight. And I helped him a lot.

"Back there on the bald range I knowed all of that country. I could start in at the Dalton Gap and name every gap from there to Silers Meadows.

"And I've conveyed worlds of people back in that mountain – hikers, sightseers going in there to see that. I had two mules and a burro and I'd get more horses.

"I'd take just gangs of people back in there, and sometimes spend the night with them. And sometimes I'd take them up there and they'd stay a week or 10 days.

"I'd take my team and I'd go over to Riverside (near Townsend) and haul their grub, their supplies over, and pack 'em out to the mountain. And I'd go after the people and carry them out again."

The fall of the year was McCaulley's favorite season.

CARVING animals of the Smokies in wood from real life was one of the natural talents of mountain man John McCaulley. The picture was made in 1960 at his latter-day home near Maryville, a year before his death at the age of 81.

"Along when the leaves began to turn brown then we'd want to hunt wild game, you know. We'd want to go to the mountain, and camp out, and hear the katydids holler, right coarse!

"That's when we done our big hunting, was in the fall and early winter."I used to trap for bear, me and my brother did, away back yonder on the Defeat (Ridge) and Thunderhead. We had traps set out there. We'd go to our traps and turkey-hunt.

"I guess I've killed more wild turkeys than ever another man living in the state of Tennessee."

Did the bears come into Cades Cove much?

"No, the bear didn't come in. We was too hot after them. We kept them on the back streets, back there. We'd go after them in November and put them back.

"But there was lots of turkeys, lots of squirrels, and we had pretty plenty of deer. We had pretty plenty of game there, but not like our forefathers, I don't guess.

"And we had plenty of fish. I could step out from my house with the kids and in two hours get a nice mess of trout fish for supper.

"But you can't do it now for there ain't nothin' there for the fish to live on. And there never will be any fish in them streams for there ain't nothin' for them to live on.

"When you took the cattle out of that mountain, and you took the hogs out of that mountain, you took all the fish food out.

"The worms'd be in the cattle stools, and the hogs'd root them into the branches, and they'd wash into the creeks, and the fish done well (on the worms).

"The hogs run wild in the woods. Put a bell on the old sow and turn her out, with her litter, and go see about her along.

"And then in the fall of the year we'd drive them in just as fat as if they was in the cornfield. The acorns hit (fell) and the chestnuts hit and, law, it wasn't no trouble to drive in a big herd of fat hogs.

"In the fall we'd separate into families and go to the mountain and tend to our hogs, move'm along from place to place where the chestnuts was plentiful.

"I saw one time, in the cabin at the bald mountain, 100 bushel of chestnuts, piled up there, and about four men packing off, every day. There was quite a lot of people there gathering chestnuts then.

"The last time I was ever on the mountain hunting chestnuts, me and one of the girls rode up there one day and we got up there about one o'clock. We picked up seven bushel.

"I propped them against a tree there and went back next day with the mules and carried them home and took them to Knoxville. I got four dollars a bushel for them .

"There was worlds of 'em. I'm telling you the whole *earth'd* just be black with them."

Almost everybody had apple orchards, and kept bees, and had more honey than the family could use. Beans grew wonderfully well in there. Most families raised plenty of corn for grinding into meal. Most families had enough milk cows that the springhouse was always plentifully stocked with sweet milk, butter milk and home-churned butter.

"We lived well. We didn't want for anything. We were rich and didn't know it." McCaulley said.

In praise of muley cows

In their new home they kept the language they had brought with them from Scotland. And when in later years these Scotch-Irish families moved to America in considerable numbers they brought the same language with them to the New World.

Because many of the Scotch-Irish immigrants settled on the Appalachian frontier, where other currents of civilization would seldom mingle, they were able to preserve a number of Scottish language forms.

An example is *chimley,* which is still the word that some of the older ones use when they talk about a chimney. The Lowland Scot of 400 years ago used exactly the same word, *chimley*.

Muley, a mountain adjective meaning "without horns," came from a Scottish Gaelic word that meant about the same.

The late John McCaulley, a Cades Coveite whose ancestors, at least some of them, probably came to this country from Northern Ireland, used the mountain language expressively in a 1960 interview recorded on tape. Here is a portion, almost word for word, in which McCaulley spoke of his experience with muley cows. He was 80 years

One of the McCaulley sons with the family's muley (no horns) cow at the home in Post Branch Hollow.

old at the time of the interview.

"We raised mostly beef cattle (in Cades Cove and on the bald ranges of the Smokies.)

"We had black and we had whiteface cattle, and we just had the old mountain cattle – good grade of cattle, though.

"We'd get hold of a Durham cow or a part Durham cow and we had a good milk cow. That's the main milk stock that they used in that cove. Some of them North Carolina cattle, though, was good milk cows. No question about that – they was good.

"I had one that I bought on Yellow Creek in North Carolina and raised my family on it. It was as good a cow as ever I set a bucket under.

"She was fine. She was a kind of a brindle – a roanish-looking cow with a little white stripe down her back. A muley didn't have horns and she was a natural muley (never did have horns).

"She was a fine cow and they had lots of good cattle in there. At one time a muley cow didn't bring nigh as much on the price as a cow with horns. They thought that was too bad because it didn't have no horns. Looked too ugly! They didn't want that one! No!

"My daddy bought a cow that was a fine milk cow in North Carolina one time. It was a black cow and she was a muley. He bought her for $10 and brought her home.

"And my mother just made all kinds of sport out of him. Said, 'What'd you bring that old cow here for? You know you can't never get nothin' out of her.'

"He said, 'Well, I ain't got nothin' in her. I just give $10 for her.' She was a good cow, too."

July 15, 1982

Hog or cow-brute safe with Silent Dan

Russell Whitehead knew Dan Myers personally and regards him as "one of the best mountain men who ever lived in Cades Cove."

A mountain man, in Cove language, was somebody who knew how to hunt, eat, sleep, survive and find his way home again, over unmarked trails, from the thousands of acres of wooded mountain slopes and deep hollows of the main ridge of the Smokies.

Some of these men developed their wilderness skills from looking after livestock at the crest of the Smokies, and that was true of Dan Myers, Russell says.

Dan was a herdsman who was feared by the rogue element of Smoky Mountain people. "The hog rogues would slip out in the woods and kill anybody's hogs. They'd sneak and kill your hogs when they got fat. They'd take the meat home and eat it, and more than likely waste a lot of it.

"There were people in the mountains that did the like of that. They'd make moonshine liquor for a living and some would steal any thing they could get hold of – a hog or a cow brute or anything. But

Dan Myers, a Smoky Mountain herdsman feared by the rogue element.

those people dreaded Dan Myers. They knew that if they shot any of his livestock, he'd likely put a bullet in them," Russell says.

Dan was a renter on the farm of Squire Dan Lawson, who at one time owned more land than any other Cades Cove resident. In summer Dan Myers looked after Lawson's cattle and hogs on land Lawson owned at the top of the mountain, above Mollies Ridge.

Russell remembers Myers as a silent man who seldom spoke a word he didn't have to speak. He and his wife had seven children, three daughters and four sons, and the sons were two sets of twins. The wife died relatively young and Dan never did marry again. He was content to be so free that he could go to the top of the mountain without announcing it, and stay a night or several nights to see that his cattle were secure and had adequate salt and were in an area of plentiful grass.

He would also come home unannounced. His keen knowledge of the woods allowed him to sense the approach of other people, and he would step away from the trail and stay hidden until whoever it was had passed. If it was a stranger or somebody he didn't trust, he might turn around and follow the person to see what his intention was.

Russell says that from time to time there were people who sought to test Dan by slipping up on him, but were seldom able to do it. Instead they would soon learn that Dan had somehow gotten behind them. Sometimes he would then call to them and ask what their business was, and that could be frightening.

Russell counts other skillful herders he has known, some personally and some by reputation. George Tipton and his younger brother Will, Carson Burchfield, Jim Cable, Tom Sparks and Jules Gregg were among the best – good woodsmen able to protect cattle from most of the natural forces and with the courage and diplomacy to fend off the rogues, the poachers and rustlers.

It was Carson Burchfield who told Russell about the epic bullfight on the North Carolina side of the mountain, at a place called the Rye Patch at the top of Long Hungry Ridge.

Most of the farmers who took big herds of cattle to the crest of the Smokies also took along a bull, but were careful not to have more than one bull in the same small grazing area, When two bulls did get together there might be a fight, and in that time when most cattle had horns, it could be a fight to death.

On this day that Russell tells about, a bull belonging to Dan Lawson fought one brought to the mountain by the Gamble family of Little River.

"They fought and fought, maybe for several hours," Russell says. There were trees there in the Rye Patch. Carson Burchfield was there after the fight and he said it was a sight in the world to see "how the ground was tore up." There were big logs turned over from two big bulls putting out all they had.

"Carson said Gamble's bull was bigger than Lawson's. Gamble's bull got on the upper side of Lawson's bull and pushed him under a slanting chestnut tree – had him wedged there. Then Gamble's bull ran a horn in him up at his shoulder, and Lawson's bull sank down there dead."

Russell doubts an old story that the owners of the two bulls staged the fight – brought them together intentionally. He also doubts that any herder could have stopped the fight once it started.

"I wouldn't have wanted to be nowhere near them when they fought," Russell says.

Amateur mountaineers

Some of the early settlers of Cades Cove, in the early 1800s, were so "new" at living in the mountains that they didn't know which springtime greens were poisonous and which were edible. So they followed their cattle, says Professor Henry R. Duncan. They reasoned that if they would watch what green things the cattle ate as they grazed along, then they could surely safely pick and eat the same.

Professor Duncan at the time was professor of animal husbandry at University of Tennessee, regarded as an authority on local mountains, and very much at home in the Cove.

The early Cove families worked years to establish farming as a livelihood. There was land to clear, orchards to plant, buildings to put up, a mill and dam to build to grind the grain into meal to make cornbread, the staff of life for Cove families for most of their years there.

But all those things were done in time, and Professor Duncan recalls that when he first visited Cades Cove in 1902 it was a valley of serenity and abundance.

Some of the families had several orchards, and in early September the pleasant aroma of ripe apples could be smelled throughout the valley.

There'd be two or three big sacks of freshly gathered chestnuts on every porch. The roads in the schoolhouse would he littered with hulls where the children had picked and eaten as they walked.

The ample chestnut crop of that day had even greater importance than as a family confection. The hogs ate them, and the hogs which roamed the chestnut forests surrounding the cove "got as fat as town dogs," in the words of Professor Duncan.

There were abundant gardens in summer, and cabbage, to keep and last all winter, were stored under earth and straw. Every family willing to work ate well, and without having to go to the store except maybe for salt and coffee and similar staples.

"Of course there were some few here who were trifling, and liked better to fight than to work. But for the most part the Cove families of 50 years ago were honest and industrious. The merchants who kept store here rarely ever lost a nickel on credit. Even those occasional families who moved out of the cove came back to pay their bills," says Duncan.

There have been four known churches in the Cove. Three of these still exist, and are used regularly for homecomings and meetings by their former congregations.

The oldest church is the Primitive Baptist. Its graveyard is the Cove's principal burying ground, and in it are weathered stone slabs which date back more than a century, and newer markers placed there recently.

The names of Oliver, Shields, Cable, Sparks, Gregory and others whose family histories are tied to the cove are abundant here. John Oliver, who was born in 1793, soldiered in the War of 1812, moved into Cades Cove about 1818 as its first white settler, and died there in 1864, is buried in this yard.

Russell Gregory, after whom Gregory Bald was named, was another early settler. Gregory sympathized with the Union during the Civil War. He was shot and killed in ambush in 1864 by Confederate sympathizers who came across the Smokies from North Carolina. His grave marker bears the legend, "Murdered by North Carolina Rebels."

Russell Whitehead, namesake of Russell Gregory, says his great-grandfather was killed trying to protect his cattle from bushwhackers who came into Cades Cove in 1864, during the Civil War. This stone in the cemetery of Cades Cove Primitive Baptist Church marks Gregory's grave.

Other churches still standing are the Missionary Baptist, established 1839, and the Methodist Church. There was a Methodist split during the Civil War, and the congregation which walked away from the older Methodist Church South founded a church of its own, the Methodist Church North.

There are only 11 families left in the cove now. They are "leaseholders" from the National Park Service. Most of the families whose pasts are linked to these churches have moved beyond the borders of the park.

They come back by the dozens every Decoration Day, and on warm, pleasant Sundays for the balance of each summer. They worship in the revered old buildings, and they bring baskets of food to have "dinner on the ground" afterwards.

Graves are exceptionally well kept. These are beautiful cemeteries, some of these graves decorated with longer lasting paper flowers, placed there with more reverence than if they bad been bouquets of orchids.

October 15, 1981

Cows eager to summer atop mountain

W. Wayne Oliver is of the family that lived in Cades Cove from the first white settlement until the land was taken into the new Great Smoky Mountains National Park in the 1930s.

Wayne's last step in a law career was as a judge of the Tennessee Court of Criminal Appeals. He has been retired since 1975, and he and wife Thelma live in Maryville, within view of the Smokies. These are some of Wayne's memories of a Cades Cove childhood and of ranging livestock on the high mountain meadows from Gregory Bald eastward.

Herbert M. Webster of Knoxville stood at the door of a herder's cabin he "discovered" on a Smoky Mountain hiking trip early in the 1930s. It was the log house that the John W. Oliver family of Cades Cove had built near Ekaneetlee Gap several years previously, a summer shelter for family members looking after their cattle.

"For many, many years, one or two men would lease large areas of the land on the Tennessee side of the Smokies from the Morton Butler Lumber Co., and on the North Carolina side from the Kitchen Lumber Co. They leased the land for the purpose of caring for cattle that people brought to the mountain to graze during the summer months. Most people took their cattle to the mountain early in May. The herders cared for them, kept up with them, put out salt for them.

"They charged a dollar a head if the cattle owner furnished the salt. They collected $1.25 a head for the season if they (the herders) furnished the salt and hauled it up there.

"Nominal, I would say," Wayne says as to how big a rent the herders paid the lumber companies to use the mountaintop land.

"One herder or set of herders probably looked after 500 head of cattle in a season. They would earn $500 for a summer's work, and that was a good wage then. Herders were good men, dependable, men of good judgment. I knew all of them.

"People did not send their family milk cows to the mountain, unless they were dry. We always sent a few older cows along every year, and they were anxious to go. They knew where they were going.

"The owners all had bells on their lead cattle, and the herders became familiar with the tone of each owner's bell. We also had sheep up there, and hogs. The sheep always worked along the top of the mountain. They didn't stray very far from the top.

"The whole top of the mountain, from Gregory Bald going east, for several yards down on each side of the top, was beautiful meadowland. Beautiful all along the top of the mountain – lots of grass. Of course there were large trees there, but there was no underbrush.

Did herders enjoy their work?

"It was something that had to be done," Wayne says. "There was a road from Maryville that crossed Chilhowee Mountain through where Top of the World is now, across the Flats of Chilhowee Mountain. It was called the Cooper Road. It came out into Cades Cove at the upper end of our property.

"Several of the Proffitts drove cattle in there every year, and sheep. People came from Sevier County and the whole area."

"In the late 1920s there was a period of three or four years in which there was no herder on the mountain to care for cattle. In that circumstance my father and my younger brothers built this cabin up

Hugh with the cattle.

there. The boys stayed in it during the summer months for a couple of years or more to look after the cattle.

"My brothers, Henry Clay Oliver and Hugh Oliver, and a cousin of ours, Frank Oliver, were the herd boys. I was away for all the years (late 1920s) that my family cared for its own cattle on the bald. I made many trips in earlier years."

Wayne says his cousin and brothers lived primitively in the one-room cabin which stood near the top of the mountain on the Tennessee side of the state line, three or more miles east of Gregory Bald. It was near the head of Ekaneetlee Creek, which flows into Cades Cove.

All cooking was done in the fireplace in iron kettles, frying pans or in a "baker and lid," a utensil more often called a Dutch oven. The herders were living about as simply as their Cades Cove ancestors had lived a century before.

Cattle got gaunt in the gant lot

John McCaulley lived in Cades Cove from his birth in 1880 until he moved his family out in 1937 to make way for the creation of Great Smoky Mountains National Park.

In after years, until his death at his new home south of Maryville in 1961, he was to look back on the Cades Cove years as idyllic, a long productive span that satisfied his esthetic and material needs. He spoke of Cades Cove as "a paradise" in an interview recorded in 1960.

McCaulley was the Cove's coffin maker, taking up that community obligation at the death of his father. Between them they made the coffins for probably a majority of those buried in Cades Cove's cemeteries in their time. They performed the service without asking or accepting payment.

John McCaulley was a farmer. He was a successful hunter, notably of the abundant wild turkey which fattened on the fall chestnut crop. Chestnuts were so plentiful then that they "blackened the earth" where they fell, in McCaulley's words.

He kept bees and brought his honey to Knoxville to sell on Market Square. The McCaulleys had apple trees and raised all the known vegetables of that time and place.

John cruised timber for some of the companies that began to buy timberlands in the Smokies. He would survey a tract to estimate how many board feet of this and that kind of lumber it would yield.

He raised hogs and cattle, and he looked after cattle for other owners who brought them to the grassy meadows above Cades Cove for summer grazing on Gregory Bald and Parsons Bald.

The rangers who looked after the cattle on pastures more than a mile high had a house where they lived during the grazing months, the last month of spring and all of summer.

When cattle owners drove their herds up there in the spring, from the flatlands of Blount County beyond the flanking ridges of the Smokies, they turned the cattle into a receiving lot. There were several such fenced lots convenient to the better grazing areas. These are McCaulley's words as he told why they were called "gant lots."

"When you brought your cattle up there in the spring of the year,

Visitors from Knoxville asked John and Rutha McCaulley, and their son John Earl, to stand for this picture in 1926. The son, 13, had cracked an arm in a fall from a footlog over Forge Creek.

put 'em in that lot and laid the bars up there. And you'd go down to the house and see the ranger that's down there, that's going to take care of your cattle. He'd come up to the gant lot with his book and put all them cattle down.

"How many there was – how many steers, how many heifers, how many cows, and the owner's mark." (Owners put their identifying mark on both ears of each animal. They would cut a distinctive notch in the ears or sometimes they pierced the ears with a hole of distinctive size or location.)

"Well, then, when that was done they'd turn them cattle over to the ranger and he'd drive them off to the pasture he wanted to run them in. "In the fall of the year we'd gather these cattle and put them right back in the gant lot. And they'd stay right there until they'd all be rounded up and the ranger could count out to a man all the cattle that he owned.

"They had plenty of water but nothing to eat in the gant lot. And again you'd put 500 head of cattle in there they'd have what little grass there was tromped up. If the cattle had to stay in there long they'd get gant (they'd get thin or gaunt).

"Law, our cattle's a-gantin' up awful bad in here but they'll go on good pasture when we get home. They would, too. They'd get pretty gant in there. They had plenty of water but nothing to eat, and that's why they called it the gant lot."

August 6, 1981

LATE SPRING SNOW STORM

2

Cattle crave ramps in wake of lean winter

S. Winston Henry was 11 years old in March of 1901, and it was in that month he helped his father drive 80 head of cattle across the mountains through Farr Gap, across Slickrock Creek to the slopes of Hangover Mountain, less than 15 miles southwest of Cades Cove in the Smokies.

The Henrys by now had moved into their new home on the south bank of Little Tennessee River near the mouth of Mulberry Creek, a short distance below where Chilhowee Dam stands today.

"We had a lot of cattle on hand and our feed, our grain, was getting low," Winston recalls.

"There was a man named Farr that lived in Farr Gap, which was named for his family. He had two sons who had moved into Nichols Cove below Hangover Lead, far across the valley from their dad's place.

> *"The Farr brothers sent word in March (of 1901) that the range was getting green and for my father to bring his cattle out there."*

"The sons built a cabin in there and they cleared 8 to 10 acres. They planted an orchard, raised some corn, had a garden and kept bees. They also herded cattle for my father (Pleas Henry), starting low on the mountain in early spring and moving to higher range in the warm months."

It is Winston's belief that the lumber companies already owned the entire Slickrock watershed, or most of it, although it would be another 15 years before they would move in men and machines to begin cutting its virgin timber.

Meanwhile, the owners needed to make some use of the thousands of acres of wilderness, a use that would help them keep legal possession. Winston believes his father's signed lease to range his cattle there, in season, served the owners to that end.

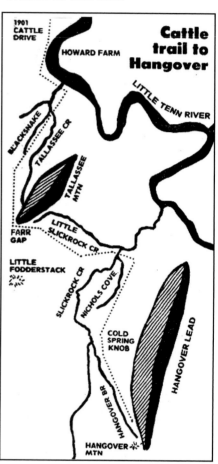

Pleas Henry in a March 1901 cattle drive left Little Tennessee River across from what was then his brother-in-law John Howard's farm and is now the village of Calderwood. He drove his 80 head of cattle up Tallassee Creek and Blacksnake Branch, climbing to Farr Gap and Little Fodderstack Mountain. He then descended its north slope into Little Slickrock to the valley of Slickrock Creek and into Nichols Cove. Trail from there crossed another ridge to Hangover Branch, to the range under mile-high Hangover Mountain. Winston Henry estimates the distance at 25 miles, possibly less. A straight line of travel would have been far shorter, he says. The Henrys did make the drive, from their farm on Little T to Hangover, in one day.

"The Farr brothers sent word in March (of 1901) that the range was getting green and for my father to bring his cattle out there.

"They charged 50 cents a head to look after them through the summer and we furnished the salt. Later on I believe they charged a dollar a head, and we still furnished the salt.

"Cattle salt was all loose salt at that time. There wasn't any block cattle salt around here. We packed it in on mules, in 100-pound sacks.

"The herders would look for a fallen tree on top of the mountain, in the area where they wanted to keep the cattle grazing. They'd cut notches into the tree and they'd pour a quart to a half-gallon of salt into each notch. The cattle wouldn't wander far from where the salt was. It helped the herders keep them in one place."

Winston says cowbells were hung on some of the lead cattle, usually on older milk cows that the other animals would follow. Sound of the bells helped the herders find the cattle at intervals, so they could inventory their numbers and their health.

The sound of the bells also helped the cattle, social animals, find one another and stay together.

A herd taken to the mountain range would be a mix of steers, heifers and cows, and in his own experience would include at least one bull. In a big herd with a considerable number of heifers of breedable age there might be several bulls.

Winston says the cattle were first taken to what was called the

Cattle trained to pull wagons, sleds, plows and to skid logs out of the woods were still common in the valley of Little Tennessee River in S. Winston Henry's youth. He was 21 or 22 years old, in 1911 or 1912, when he was photographed behind steer at right hauling firewood with a yoke of oxen and wagon borrowed from Will Orr, above Rymer Ferry, N.C. Winston at the time was a rodman with a crew of engineers surveying where Aluminum Co. of America would soon build Cheoah Dam, and firewood was for their tent camp.

"winter range" under the hemlock trees, where the dense growth was a natural roof that protected from cold rain and late snowfall.

"Back then we called those trees the *big spruce,* but now we call it *hemlock,*" Winston says. The cattle would graze just below the hemlock on ramps, lamb's tongue and other first greens of early spring.

The day in 1901 they drove the cattle up there, Pleas, his son and the Farr brothers slept under the hemlocks that night. The ramps were about six inches high and the cattle began feasting on them right away.

Winston believes it was the next day that his father pointed to a steer that had been black but now appeared to be gray in color.

"It's the ramps," Pleas told his son. People and animals that are eating ramps soon become "soaked" with the odor. In the case of the black steer the ramp smell had driven the cattle lice from its skin to the outer fringes of its hair, and there were enough of them that they gave it a gray overall color, Winston says.

August 13, 1981

Bad news from Hangover Mountain

To the north of Little Tennessee River they are called the Great Smoky Mountains; south of the river they are called the Unicoi. Except for the names they are the same Appalachian range of mountains, created in the same folding of Earth.

Pleas Henry from his farm on the south bank of the river could see the crest of the Smokies and the Unicois, and sometime past the middle of April 1901 he was concerned at how much snow he saw.

He had 80 head of cattle south of the river on Hangover Mountain, driven up there late in March. Now they were maybe trapped and hungry in snow so deep it covered their range of spring grasses, under the upper slope so steep it seems to overhang and gives the mountain its name.

Pleas Henry saddled a mule and set out for the Nichols Cove cabin of the Farr brothers, the herders who had agreed to look after the cattle for the entire grazing season of spring, summer and early fall.

Winston Henry was photographed at one end of a crosscut saw in the same mountain country from which he had helped rescue his family's hungry cattle.

The Farrs told him that some of the cattle were already dead, poisoned on the mountain ivy they found uncovered at the heads of creeks. It was the only green thing showing through snow that had fallen several days and ranged to five feet deep in places.

In the local language of the time, laurel was the word for what is now called rhododendron, and mountain ivy was the name for what is now generally called mountain laurel. It is poison to cattle that eat it. It sickens and often kills them.

Pleas hurried home and started himself and his sons chopping ears of corn, husk included, with hand axes. They chopped it into nubbins an inch or two long, small enough for a cow to chew. Cattle aren't equipped to chew on a whole, hard ear of corn, Winston Henry says.

Winston became 11 years old in March of 1901. Now, a month later, while his father and brothers were chopping corn, he was told to saddle two mules and to put horse collars on both mules.

Tie the saddles to the collars, Winston was told, so the saddles will not slip backward on the steep mountain trails, under the heavy load of corn and rider they will be carrying. They were not pack saddles. They were common riding saddles, Winston says.

The snowfall that covered the higher mountains to such great depth left only four inches on the Henry farm beside the river, but it was enough to kill their first planting of corn that was already in leaf when snow and temperature both fell.

The corn had to be planted again right away, so Pleas and his older sons, Lloyd and Bruce, stayed home to do that. Winston was chosen to travel across the mountain alone, riding one mule and leading the other, to carry feed to the hungry cattle. If he could reach the Farr brothers' cabin in one day, some of the cattle might still be saved.

"If you get lost, give that mule his head (free rein) and he'll find his way back to the barn," Pleas Henry said in farewell advice. "The mules were as old as I was, and they knew their way through all those mountains," Winston says today.

Four big sacks of corn were loaded onto the back of the trailing mule, and two sacks onto the one Winston was riding. The snow was so deep at the higher places, at Farr Gap and down Stiffknee Ridge, that the collars of both mules plowed into it.

Distance from the Henry farm to the Farr cabin in Nichols Cove, a tributary of Slickrock Creek, was about 18 miles and a one-way trip through the snow required most of a day, Winston recalls. He made three round trips in six days, and at the end of that time the snow had melted enough that the grasses in the cattle range were beginning to show again.

The Farrs skinned the hides from all the dead cattle they could find and put the hides into burlap sacks for Winston to take home on the backs of the mules each trip. The hides were sold to a tannery, he says. The carcasses were left to lie and rot, carrion for the wildcat, opossum, crow and buzzard.

Map merges 1901 landmarks with those of Great Smoky Mountains National Park created in the years since. Heavy shaded line shows route of the April 1901 cattle drovers from Dry Valley to Spence Field and return. Their trail through Schoolhouse Gap and across Turkeypen Ridge crossed Laurel Creek where the tourist road into Cades Cove now threads. Final part of the climb to Spence Field and neighboring Russell Field was the historic path up Bote Mountain. Thunderhead, adjoining Spence Field, is more than 5500 feet high.

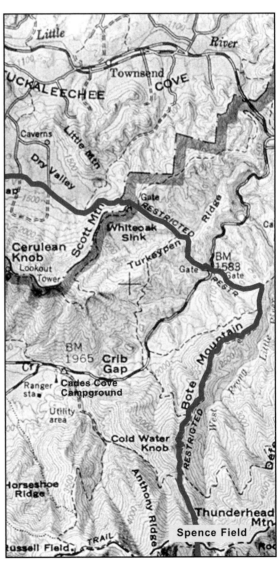

At the end of a week, 40 head of cattle, half the herd, had been rescued from cold and hunger. Winston's recollection is that most of the 40 survived and fattened the rest of the grazing season, until the Henrys went back to Hangover Mountain to round them up again in October before another snow would fall.

August 20, 1981

Drovers live to tell of herd's death in snow

There are still a few among us, in 1981, who remember the
April 1901 storm that left five feet or more of snow on the
higher ridges of the Smokies and Unicoi Mountains to
the south. We began with Winston Henry's account of his
family's loss of 40 head of cattle on Hangover Mountain.
We move now to the Bald Range of the Smokies, above
Cades Cove, for another memory of the same snow.

Charles Snider Dunn was second-youngest of 16 children of
William Hurst Dunn and Dorotha Catherine Dunn. Of the 16, Charles

**Squire William H. Dunn
and wife Dorotha Catherine
Snider Dunn sat for formal
portrait sometime early in
the century, but several
years after they gave
shelter to more than a
dozen men trapped in a
Smoky Mountain snow-
storm in 1901. The Dunns
and their 16 children lived
in Dry Valley in Blount
County, beside a trail that
led from Little River to
Spence Field.**

and one sister, Queenie Dunn Myers, survive today. Charles was nearly
8 years old and aware of the human adventure of the late-season snow-
storm of the third week of April 1901.

The Dunns lived in Dry Valley, caverned hollow at the edge of what is now Townsend, beside the historic trail to the crest of the Smokies at Spence Field.

Their big home for many years had been a stopping place for cattle drovers, most from Blount and nearby sections of Knox and Sevier counties, driving herds to summer range in the grassy forests at the shoulder of the mountain, to fatten there at almost no cost.

"We always turned our own cattle on the mountain about April 10. The spring greens, the lamb's tongue and crowsfoot, were up by then, and the cattle thrived on that. Most owners tried to get their herds to the mountain by the middle of April," Charles says.

It was near that date in 1901 that more than 100 head, maybe more than 200, were driven to the Dunn place to be corralled for the

A.J. "Jack" Fisher, left, of Maryville and Henry McMillan of Knoxville were photographed at Spence Field in 1935, the summer after the last cattle, sheep and horses were allowed to graze on the "bald" or treeless meadows of the Smokies. Camera was in the hands of Knoxvillian Carlos C. Campbell. All three people involved with the picture are deceased. Jack Fisher in 1935 was superintendent of the Cades Cove CCC camp.

night. These were cattle owned by the Love, Sharp, Davenport and Maxey families of south Knox County, and by Sam Davis, a Dunn relative from Hubbard in Blount County.

Some of the people involved had come to Dry Valley ahead of the drive and bought and hauled hay to the Dunn barn for feeding the cattle during the one-night layover.

Some of the owners also had fancy, custom-made leather muzzles to put on their cattle for the rest of the journey, to keep them from eating the poisonous mountain laurel along the trail at higher elevations ahead. The muzzles had hung in the Dunn barn since the end of the last grazing season.

Pat Dunn

"Some of those people didn't believe in putting all that money into leather muzzles," Charles says. "Some of them made their muzzles by peeling pawpaw bark. They worked about as well but didn't last nearly as long."

The cattle had what would be their last good feeding before they were turned out of the corral next morning for the last day of the drive, through Schoolhouse Gap and finally to the environs of Spence Field on the main ridge of the Smokies.

Most of the cattle would soon be dead in the cold and deep snow that reached the top of the mountain about the same time.

Charles' s older brother, Pat Dunn, more than 16 years old in April of 1901, was asked at the final hour to join the drive because of his considerable knowledge of that part of the Smokies. There was a slight rain falling, and other more ominous weather signs.

Charles in years to come would hear the story many times from his brother. "As they got up the mountain it got colder," he says.

"They corralled their cattle up there and all of them froze to death. All except one little knotty-head yearling. It stayed down around the herd cabin and survived."

The Journal and Tribune: Tuesday, April 23, 1901

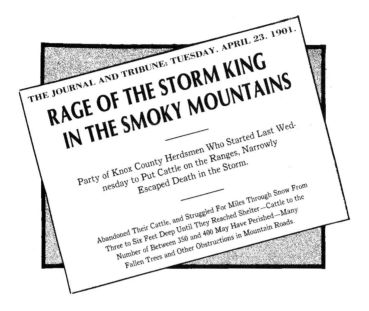

THE JOURNAL AND TRIBUNE: TUESDAY, APRIL 23, 1901.

RAGE OF THE STORM KING IN THE SMOKY MOUNTAINS

Party of Knox County Herdsmen Who Started Last Wednesday to Put Cattle on the Ranges, Narrowly Escaped Death in the Storm.

Abandoned Their Cattle, and Struggled For Miles Through Snow From Three to Six Feet Deep Until They Reached Shelter—Cattle to the Number of Between 350 and 400 May Have Perished—Many Fallen Trees and Other Obstructions in Mountain Roads.

The first news to the outside world about the late winter snow storm in the Smoky Mountains was carried by the Journal and Tribune newspaper under the headline reconstructed above.

While the Associated Press dispatches from various cities in the north have been full of startling news concerning the recent storm, there have been tidings from the Smoky Mountains of Blount County of the nature to indicate that the force of the storm was nowhere more terribly felt than there.

These tidings were brought in by Ben Sharp, Jasper Kerner, of Sevier county: He and Matt Davenport, Tony Luttrell and the Love brothers, of Knox County, who on last Wednesday started to the mountains with a number of cattle to put them on the ranges for the summer and fall.

They relate a desperate call for their lives. They were caught in the grip of the storm in the fastness of the mountains, several miles from habitation. On the bleak tops of the mountains they left their huddled and freezing cattle and obeying the injunction of old herdsmen, hurried out of the mountains for their lives. The party struggled through snow from three to six feet deep until their horses were exhausted and then dismounting struggled on afoot through a blinding storm, themselves nearly exhausted and famished before they reached the first houses and obtained food and shelter. This haven of refuge was the home of Squire Dunn in Dry Valley. At this place was a band of land surveyors driven in by the storm, who had been in the mountains surveying lands which Pennsylvania capitalists bought recently. This party came into Knoxville yesterday and one of them furnishes the following facts of what happened:

As the cattlemen were expecting feed for their stock, of course they made no provision for anything of this sort and really very scanty provision for themselves and their horses and mules. The storm overtook them, blowing a great gale uprooting and breaking off the brush and trees and continuing until they were almost entirely submerged in snow. The herders on the mountains becoming alarmed, they concluded to try to escape. This they found almost impossible. Their horses and mules were covered with a thick coat of ice; they themselves were about famished; cattle were dead and dying.

When they started down the mountain the horses and mules were unable to travel or find their way. They turned them loose and with great difficulty succeeded in getting off the mountain after wading through snow to their waists for ten or twelve hours. They finally landed at Squire Dunn's in Dry Valley on Saturday evening, where everything was done to make them comfortable. Many of them had lost their hats and, in fact, all of them had lost all their blankets and everything of this sort that was not really fastened to their bodies. In the gale of wind, sleet and snow it was impossible for them to get off the mountain and carry anything with them.

After they obtained something to eat and had thawed out at Squire Dunn's, they were able to relate, in a disconnected way, their experience. They did not seem to worry much about their losses, nor anything of that sort, but seemed to be more thankful that they had escaped with their lives.

Squire Dunn's house, being crowded with a lot of surveyors who are now doing work on the mountain, he was unable to give them shelter for the night, other than lying on the floor, so resorting to a school director near by, his kind offices were obtained in securing for them the school house, in which a good fire was made and they were soon very comfortable, and, with a little foraging in the community, plenty of everything was gotten together to make them comfortable.

Sunday morning, the water still being very high on the Little River, the party started for Knoxville, and succeeded in getting here.

In crossing Little River in most places the men had to swim the horses and let the wagons float. They took care, however to have a good pilot at each of the fordings, who was thoroughly familiar with the local conditions.

"On the way back from Gamble's to Knoxville, the query of almost every farmer was, 'Why didn't you bring your cattle off?' The only answer that could be made as they hadn't time to stop en route was: "If you had been there you wouldn't ask such a foolhardy question."

On the mountains there were between 350 and 400 cattle, all of which may now be dead.

On taking up the cattle to the top of the mountain some of the less hardy ones became exhausted along the way and were tied to trees and left behind. In returning all of these were found dead and encrusted with ice and snow. When the party left the mountains Sunday the snow was still falling.

They found many trees and obstructions in the roads. Many telephone poles in Tuckaleechee and Miller's Cove were down and one horse was severely cut by getting tangled in the fallen wires.

1901 snow ended cattle drives from Knox

Charles Snider Dunn continues a recollection of the deep,
late-season snow in which cattle herds froze to death
on the mile-high crest of the Smokies in April 1901.
Charles was 8 years old when it happened and
lived beside it and through it.

Charles Dunn says the snow was so deep on the upper mountain that only the tops of the posts could be seen in the gant lot, the corral or enclosure where herder Tom Sparks received the cattle for counting.

He says the drovers, including his brother Levi Paterson "Pat" Dunn, stayed in the little herder's cabin with Sparks, west of Spence Field and on the North Carolina side.

"They were about to freeze to death in that old log cabin. They cut a tree and put one end in the fireplace with the other end through the open door.

"They stuck it out three nights in the cabin. Tom was about out of provisions by then, so they decided to get out. They were all on horseback but the snow was so deep the horses would fight it. They had to dismount and walk and break the way themselves, until they got down to Bote mountain," Charles says.

When they reached the Dunn home in Dry Valley its nine rooms already were filled with family and another group of stranded men, a party of surveyors headed by W.B. Townsend.

The snowfall caught the surveyors while they were looking at timberlands recently acquired on West Prong of Little River, which heads up under Spence Field. Townsend, from Pennsylvania, was president of the new Little River Lumber Co., and within a few months the nearby village of Townsend, in Tuckaleechee Cove, would be named for him.

Charles says his father, Squire William Dunn, had a key to neigh-

41

boring Red Bank School in Dry Valley and that there was a good supply of firewood piled there. He sent some of his children to start a fire in the big iron heating stove.

Others gathered bedding, quilts and straw pallets to lay on the floor, and Squire then sent some of the overflow of guests to the schoolhouse to spend the night.

He kept the cattle drovers, the last group to arrive, in the home, Charles says. All were suffering from the cold and most hadn't eaten much in recent days. The horses and mules they rode were painfully hungry, and the Dunn children took them to the barn and saw immediately to their needs.

Most of the drovers were cattle owners from Knox and Sevier counties, or men who worked for them. Their intention Wednesday, April 17, had been to drive the cattle to the gant lot west of Spence

Home of the Dry Valley Dunns looked like this before it burned in 1980, and looked not much different 80 years before. Cattle drovers trapped several days in deep snow on the crest of the Smokies above Cades Cove found shelter here on the evening of April 20, 1901. The Dunn home was the first they came to after struggling off the mountain. This is the road they traveled, and they first saw the house from this approach.

Field, to deliver them to herder Tom Sparks to look after for the next five months or more.

The drovers had not much food with them, nor feed for their horses and mules. Their plan had been to start back down the mountain next morning.

But snow began to fall before they reached the top of the Smokies on Wednesday, and with it came a wind that toppled trees and blew away some of the drovers' hats and the blankets some of them wrapped

Cattle digging through snow to find grass underneath.

around themselves in the unexpected cold. Charles's brother Pat was one who came home without a hat.

Snow continued to fall until it lay four feet in places and deeper in drifts. Temperature at top of the mountain was still below freezing when they headed out Saturday, but by now, without provisions, there was a greater danger in staying.

Many of the cattle were already dead from cold and lack of feed, although they had been penned so they could huddle for warmth. The deep snow now covered the grass that would have sustained them, and to turn the cattle out of the corral would let them at the poison laurel, which also would have killed them.

To buy cattle in the spring, to hire drovers to take them to the mountain range, to buy a summer supply of cattle salt and to pay the herder at least some of his fee in advance amounted to a capitalist undertaking, Charles says.

An owner expected to recover his investment plus a profit when he brought fatter cattle off the mountain that fall and sold them to the meat packers. But the 1901 snow that cost them their herds, about 450 head in the Spence Field range alone, discouraged the Knox County owners. They never again brought cattle to that part of the Smokies, Charles says.

Russell Whitehead was 13 years old and living in Cades Cove in 1901. "I was working for my first cousin, Frank Wilson. He had half a big farm rented, and I was just a big old boy, big enough to plow with a double-shovel plow. I was with him when it came that snow.

"I remember George Sparks came off the mountain, somebody with him. They had a big mule that belonged to somebody up on Ellejoy Creek. He said they brought the mule along to break the snow, to make a trail.

"They said the snow on top was breast-deep, but not as deep when they got down to Ledbetter Ridge."

"Frank Wilson, the man I was working for, had 20 head of young cattle. When the snow melted off we took the cattle to Spence Field, and stayed all night in the Spence cabin.

"The dead cattle was laying out there then. I seen them with my own eyes. I figured about 400 of them dead, but other people said about 450 died.

"That was the biggest snow I've ever seen and it fell the 19th night and 20th day of April, 1901. People talked about it for years, but me and Winston Henry may be about the only two people left living that remember it real well."

We know some of the names of those who were on the ill-fated 1901 drive, and together were the owners of 200 head. They included:

Matt and Hugh Davenport, Samuel and Walter Love and William Thomas, who lived near Knoxville, Jeff and William Sharp of Trundles Crossroads, A. Jasper "Jap" Keener of Boyds Creek.

Greer's oxen died swift as lightning

In the 94 years Russell Whitehead has lived, he remembers a few Cades Cove farmers, but not many, who yoked oxen as work animals to plow fields, pull farm sleds and wagons, and snake timber out of the woods.

These were domestic cattle. They were bull calves that were castrated and allowed to mature as steers. Then if they were of promising size and strength they were spared from being slaughtered for meat and were trained as work animals, usually in pairs.

Early in the Smoky Mountain frontier they were the most common work stock. "But that was before my time. It was mostly mules and horses by the time I was born," Russell says.

Pastures became thin in the dry months of summer, and to save what little grass there was for the family cow, many families turned their work stock loose in the woods as soon as the crops were in.

"My mother's uncle, Andy Greer, had a yoke of oxen. He turned them out in the woods and they drifted up to the top of the mountain.

"It came a storm and those two old oxen and a herd of cattle, 15 to 20 head, huddled on top of a knob under some trees. Lightning hit some of the trees and killed all that herd of cattle, including Uncle Andy's oxen.

"That knob is on the North Carolina side of the mountain at the head of Twentymile Ridge. And it's been called Greer Knob ever since Andy Greer's oxen were killed there," Russell says.

(The Appalachian Trail from the main ridge of the Smokies south to Fontana now skirts Greer Knob.)

Russell and his younger brother Frank, when they were teen-agers early in the century, tried a summer season at herding cattle high on the mountain. They stayed in a cabin east of Gregory Bald and south of Rich Gap, on the North Carolina side.

Their father, Taylor Whitehead, thought they might be young for the job. So he went up there and stayed with them for a time, to see

45

how much herder's lore they knew and whether he could quit being concerned about their safety.

They all went down Twentymile Creek to a place called Twentymile Flats, where they had cattle grazing in several grassy pockets. They located all their cattle and put out salt for all of them, and began the walk back up the mountain to the cabin.

"It came a storm, one of the worst lightning storms I've ever been in, and all three of us were scared. I thought to myself that it was just such a storm that killed Andy Greer's oxen," Russell says.

He says that cattle become as frightened of lightning as do humans, and that when cattle are on high ground in a storm they will run crashing for the hollows.

"But not always in time. Lightning killed a lot of cattle and sheep at the top of the mountain," Russell says.

Cattle, like humans in another regard, were more comfortable on the ridges in hot weather. They enjoyed the breezes and cooler temperatures of the higher altitude, Russell says.

He says he has often thought that the cattle killed on Greer Knob were enjoying life a short while earlier, lying in the shade on a hot day, chewing their cuds, until one great bolt of lightning killed all of them and splintered several trees.

Through the years there must have been people killed by the fiercer lightning at the top of the mountain, but Russell says he doesn't remember any instances.

He says that Fonz Cable, whom he ranks with the most able of the livestock herders, "probably made more tracks on Smoky than any other man that ever lived," and survived the lightning.

Fonz was also a bear hunter who in his lifetime guided dozens of hunting treks to Thunderhead Mountain. But most of those expeditions were in November, when the danger of being trapped in early, heavy snow was greater than the peril of lightning.

Fonze Cable's son Robert "Buster" Cable was 12 years old when Fonze began using him as a helper in organized hunts. Robert's role was to be "on stand" or to stay in a place through which the bear might try to escape the hunters.

On his 87th birthday in October of 2000, Robert remembered

back 75 years to his first time on stand. He was carrying a 12-gauge shotgun loaded with buckshot and holding it in a way that would let him be on target quickly if a bear came along.

No bear did come his way that day but there was a low-pitched whistling sound mournful in the wind that blows without letup on and around Thunderhead. Then Robert discovered that when he moved the shotgun so that the muzzle was not at right angle to the wind, the whistling stopped.

Lightning killed sheep, sundered giant trees

Coax a skillful mule-driver to go along and a 1920s camping trip to Thunderhead Mountain was more likely to be free of trouble. "The Bote Mountain trail was a steep one and not meant for wagon travel," says Ernest Tipton. "Mules got tired at the end of the climb and it took somebody that knew how to make a mule move.

"I was too easy with them and the mules knew it," Ernest says. The one small wagon pulled by the mules carried the tent and heavy poles, cooking and eating utensils and food for two or three dozen people for a week sometimes.

It hauled the homemade quilts and blankets that were a mountain camper's bedding long before sleeping bags became commonplace. It carried axes for cutting firewood and tools for repairing the wagon if it broke along the way or lost a wheel.

Campers on horseback might reach the mountaintop first, but the setting up of camp before dark awaited the arrival of the wagon. So the Tipton and Emert families felt more certain of pitching camp in time if Herman Hodge or John Headrick, or the brothers Mose and Sam Everett, agreed to drive the mules.

"Then after they rested a day or two we'd put bridles on the mules and ride them bareback. We'd ride up to Laurel Top and Rocky Top, or to Russell Field in the other direction," Ernest says.

"Fred Latham and I rode the mules over toward Russell Field one evening to pick ripe sarvis berries. We sat on the mules and reached up and picked the berries off the tree branches and ate them as we picked them. Sarvis berries have a pleasant, cherry-like taste, as I remember them. The trees grow among other timber at higher levels.

"We'd eaten our fill and picked some to take back to camp when we saw a storm coming," Ernest continued. "So we hurried the mules hack to Tom Sparks' cabin, which was close to our camp.

"Tom Sparks was living then and he'd let us crowd in there when it stormed. Inside the cabin we felt safer from lightning, but whether we were safer I don't know.

"This day after picking sarvis we had just reached the cabin when the storm did, too. Usually we tethered the mules to trees near the tent, but this time we tied them to the cabin. And during the storm those trees were burst all to pieces by lightning. That's the same trees where the mules would have been tied ordinarily."

Ernest's sister Belle and Belle's husband Ira Emert were along on that camping trip, known to have been before 1926 because of the fact Tom Sparks was alive. The longtime livestock herder was killed at his cabin in 1926 in a circumstance not fully understood by those who remember it.

Belle says the storm that Ernest remembers is the same lightning storm that killed 27 sheep in a flock of 30 on Spence Field. The sheep belonged to Jim Martin, a Walland farmer who ranged both cattle and sheep on mountain pastures.

In memory of cattle that climbed mountains

Jim Long likes to sit on his back porch because it gives him a view of Chilhowee Mountain. Jim has driven cattle across that rampart many times in former years, and on through Cades Cove to summer pastures high in the Smokies.

We found Jim on the porch the day we visited. We pulled up a chair and sat beside him in the warm fall sunshine and listened as he harked back to cattle-driving days. A long time ago it was, for Jim is now 77 years old.

The drive would start in the spring, sometime in April after the thaw in the low country. Farmers from Crooked Creek, where Jim then lived, tried to put their cattle into one herd for the drive.

They'd start at early morning with pockets full of biscuits and other vittles prepared at home. Some farmers fed grain to their cattle for several days before the start of the drive, so the brutes too would have the strength to make the long hard climb.

Across Chilhowee they'd start – pulling, pushing, coaxing, yelling at the slow animals. Most herds traveled what was known as the Cooper Road, but it was more a trail than a road in stretches. Even with good luck it would be late afternoon when they reached the cove, and late evening when they finally made it to the heights at the herder's cabin just under Gregory Bald.

There'd often be snow at that height at that time of spring. Jim remembers one trip when snow in the air was so thick they could see only a few feet ahead. George Tipton greeted them from his cabin door and bade them come in and warm themselves. "And then we'll take the cattle down below the snow," he said.

"I thought to myself, 'Where's that going to be?' I thought it was snowing all over the world," Jim recalls today.

The drivers would generally stay all night at the cabin before starting back to their homes and farms the next morning. Owners paid Tipton 75 cents for every animal left in his charge for the summer. Each also furnished cattle salt, or else gave the herdsman nine cents a head to buy it. The prices Jim remembers are probably from the 1880s or 1890s. They became higher as the 20th Century approached.

George Tipton and his family were among several in the business of looking after cattle, sheep, and hogs brought to the mountain for summer range. The sheep generally stayed on the highest, grassiest part of the balds and kept the grass eaten down so close that the cattle would forage elsewhere – down into the forest slopes. It was the herder's job to see that they didn't stray from a certain boundary of land. To go down every so often and drive them back toward the heights. To see that they were salted every week or so.

Came September and the owners would hike back to the bald to round up their cattle and start the drive home. Locating the animals in the vast forest was often difficult. Sometimes it meant walking far down into the hollows on the North Carolina side, almost to where Fontana Lake now lies. The streams that fall and tumble off that slope make a lot of noise so that it was hard to hear a cowbell, and a searcher might walk within a few feet of an animal without seeing or hearing it. There were times when cattle disappeared completely – never again were seen by their owners.

As the cattle were located they were herded into an enclosure such as the old "gant lot" in the gap east of Gregory Bald. There they were kept to work off their bloat or until an owner found the last of his herd. Then the trek home started.

On the downhill trip it wasn't as hard to keep the cattle moving as it was to keep them from straying into ravines and hollows along the way. On the upward journey – that's when a driver's patience was tried.

When Jim was a very young man one of his neighbors gave him advice that he used with great success the first time a stubborn steer lay down and refused to budge. He walked around and got below the steer, and dropped to all fours and unrolled his new rain slicker and draped it over himself.

Then Jim crawled toward the animal. One look at that strange crawling creature with the glossy hide and the steer leaped to its feet and was soon at the head of the herd.

Who were some of the men who drove cattle to the mountain range in those long ago days? There were hundreds, but Jim recalls these few: Tip Davis, Jim Reese Davis, Bud Hitch, Doc Waters, Enoch Waters, John White, Snyder Feezell, and Fayte Hall.

October 22, 1981

MOUNTAINS POSED BOTH BENEFITS AND PERILS

3

Staggerweed poisoned livestock and people

W. Wayne Oliver of Maryville recalls his family ranging livestock on the crest of the Smokies in the warm months and of driving them down the mountain to the Oliver farm in Cades Cove as cold weather approached.

"Cattle gathering day was Labor Day, the first Monday in September every year. About a week prior to that time the herders would gather in all the cattle into a large field that was called the *gant lot.*

"It was given that name because when several hundred head of cattle were corralled in a space of a few acres, they very quickly ate all the available grass and lost a few pounds. Gaunt was the word. They became gaunt, but it was pronounced gant, locally.

"The first Monday in September, the owners would go to the mountain. The herders would separate out your cattle, and you would start down the trail toward Cades Cove with them. Five minutes later they would separate out my cattle and I would start down the trail with them."

The Cades Cove farmers would always make it home off the mountain the first day, Wayne says. Those who lived beyond the cove would camp there for the night and continue their drive the next day, he says.

"Cattle driven off the mountain were always corralled for the night in Uncle Noah Burchfield's great meadow. He was a neighbor of ours, across the road from our property. A lot of cattle came down with a mysterious disease after the first day's drive. People back then called it the *milk sick.* I've seen a number of cattle that died of it there, in

53

Uncle Noah's meadows, and had to be disposed of. It went on as long as there were cattle in the mountains," Wayne says.

Milk sick or milk sickness was a serious ailment, of cattle and of humans, in only a few parts of the country in Wayne's childhood. It was a scourge in the Smokies, especially among cattle grazing at higher elevations. People who drank the milk of an afflicted cow often became ill.

Symptoms of milk sickness were headache, loss of appetite, fatigue, nausea, excessive thirst, constipation and foul breath. People and livestock more often recovered, but death was also common. When death resulted, it came in a few days, and was preceded by convulsions and coma. Abraham Lincoln's mother, Nancy Hanks, is believed to have died of milk sickness.

There are people wise to the Smokies who believe that the mysterious deer deaths in Cades Cove several years ago were caused by milk sickness. Deer, sheep and cattle are all prey to it. As to the cause of milk sickness, Smoky Mountain people for generations believed it was caused by their livestock eating a poisonous plant, although they didn't always know which plant it was.

W. Wayne Oliver, now a retired judge of the Tennessee Court of Criminal Appeals, was photographed in Cades Cove more than 60 years ago with his father's prize Angus bull, Old Black Joe. Wayne's father was John W. Oliver, who introduced the first purebred cattle ever brought into the Cove in herd quantity. The expensive bull was kept on the Oliver farm and was never exposed to the perils of the open summer range high on the crest of the Smokies.

Now we know, says R. Glenn Cardwell, who was born in Greenbrier Cove of the Smokies slightly more than 50 years ago. Glenn today is a naturalist on the Great Smoky Mountains National Park interpretive staff at Sugarlands Visitor Center, near Gatlinburg.

The plant that caused the ailment was and is *white snakeroot,* a

R. Glenn Cardwell, Smokies native and a naturalist on the interpretive staff at Sugarlands Visitor Center, shows a stalk of leaves and flowers of white snakeroot that is common above the 3,000-foot level in the Smokies. It once was a cause of sickness and death of livestock that ate its leaves. Humans also became ill when they drank the milk of cattle poisoned by the weed. The affliction came in late summer and early fall.

species of *eupatorium.* In Glenn's Smoky Mountain neighborhood it was commonly called *staggerweed* because of the behavior of livestock after they ate the leaves.

Glenn says *white snakeroot* grows at higher elevations, and is abundant along the mile-high road from Newfound Gap to Clingmans Dome. It also flourishes in damp, shaded hollows at lower elevations.

Glenn supposes that cattle coming off the mountain, hungry from a day or more in the gant lot without feed or water, nibbled at anything green along the trail.

Most local people knew to keep their cattle away from *white snakeroot* and other poisonous plants. Cattle owners from beyond the cove didn't always know the local lore, and it was they whose cattle were most likely to sicken and sometimes die.

Pioneer trout rode to cove in wagons

*W. Wayne Oliver recalls his farm childhood in Cades Cove,
and his family's early pioneering there, well before
the creation of Great Smoky Mountains National Park.
Wayne's parents were Nancy Ann Whitehead
and John W. Oliver.*

"About 1905 or 1906, Morton Butler from Chicago, one of the owners of the Morton Butler Lumber Co. tract of land on the Tennessee side of the Smokies in front of Cades Cove, was at his summer cabin on Post Creek near the Parson Branch Road. He would ride toward the Cove and meet my father, and they would ride toward the Chestnut Flats and back.

"In the course of those conversations, Butler asked my father about fish in the mountain streams. At that time there were no trout except a few brook trout, which got there by some mysterious way, and a few hornyheads and suckers.

"Butler told my father that if he would contact his congressman, the government would furnish fingerlings to stock those streams with rainbow trout free of charge.

"So in 1907, Henry R. Gibson, who wrote *Gibson's Suits in Chancery,* still the bible of chancery court practice in Tennessee, was in Congress. My father contacted him and as a result of that, in 1907, the year I was born, they sent a shipment of fingerling rainbows down to Townsend from the hatchery at Greeneville. They came to the railhead at Townsend.

"The station agent had to write a postcard notifying that the fish were there, and my father had to get a bunch of wagons over there to get them. By the time all that transpired the day for release of the trout, stamped on the barrels, had arrived.

"So the station agent, Uncle Enos Coulter, got somebody to help him and they carried the barrels of trout across the road and dumped

56

them into Little River. And that was the first rainbow trout ever in Little River.

"The next year they coordinated it better. The wagons got over there in time and they got the fish into Cades Cove. They put them into Abrams Creek along the meadows there, and some in Post Creek out toward the Parsons Branch area.

"The people of the Cove looked askance at that experiment. They said it was another of John Oliver's new-fangled ideas, like thoroughbred chickens and sheep.

"When spring rains come all those fish will be washed over Abrams Falls and nobody will ever hear of them any-more. This was the speculation, and with that the whole idea was dismissed.

"I want a picture of you with your bee shed," a family member said to the late John W. Oliver one day. Oliver introduced the purebred strain of bees into Cades Cove and housed them beside and under this special shed. Each hive was suspended to be clear of the ground, so that ants could not get into the honey. The bees were three-banded Italian honeybees.

"Of course all that water was virgin water, you know. Plenty of fish feed of all kind in the streams. Nobody paid any attention to the experiment any more until three years had passed.

"The third spring at spawning time, in early April, trout were going upstream to spawn, up every little stream to spawn. And it was suddenly discovered that the streams were just full of big rainbow trout.

"The word went out and people came from every direction to fish (about 1911 or 1912). I can remember seeing those fish in the streams.

Tremendous trout. People dynamited and seined them. Fishermen just flocked in there, like they do when there's good fishing anywhere.

"The fish were depleted then. There was some restocking done in the early 1930s when Charlie Dunn was ranger of the East Tennessee side of the park. (Charlie's wife, Lucille, is Wayne Oliver's sister.)

"They had rearing pools at the Chimneys and at the upper end of Cades Cove, all built with Civilian Conservation Corps labor. They did some restocking.

"But the official policy of the National Park Service now is not to make much effort to restock, although there are over 600 miles of prime trout streams in the park."

Mailman's horse wary of rotten bridges

W. Wayne Oliver remembers the Cable Mill, now operated by the National Park Service as a living museum of life in the Smokies. It is the mill that is seen today by most Cades Cove visitors.

Wayne was born in 1907 and probably was younger than 10 years old at the time of his first solo ride to mill.

"There were only two grist mills, corn mills, in the Cove in my lifetime. One was the Cable Mill. It was there that I first went to mill alone," Wayne says. "I rode a little bay horse named Tyson that my father owned. He bought Tyson from Gen. L. D. Tyson of Knoxville.

"Tyson had fallen through so many rotten bridges, carrying my father on his mail route, that nobody could ride him across a bridge except my father, and only then by putting the spurs to him.

"So I had to get off and lead Tyson across a bridge and get back on. In doing so I got my sack of corn a little sideways in the saddle. When I got to the mill and slid off, the corn slid off on top of me. I remember that very distinctly.

"The miller was Uncle Jim Cable. There was a bell there that you rang if he wasn't already at the mill. He would come as soon as he could walk the distance from his house down to the mill, maybe 500 or 600 yards.

"When your grist was almost ready, when your sack of corn was almost ground and he was ready to sack up your meal, he'd say 'Son, get your nag'.

"You'd lead your horse alongside a block. He had two cuts off a large poplar tree, cuts of different height. He could step off the walkway onto the first one, and then step to the top one, and from there he could easily put your sack of meal onto your horse.

"In the wintertime he had a fire going all the time in that little warming shed you've seen in early pictures of the mill. People could wait there with a degree of comfort while their corn was being ground," Wayne says.

His father John W. Oliver owned many good saddle horses through the years, most of them bought for use on his 24-mile daily circuit of the Cades Cove mail route.

Oliver is believed to have been the only rural mail carrier Cades Cove ever had, from the beginning of rural free delivery late in the 19th Century until he retired in 1937, after most Cove inhabitants had departed and after the Cove had formally become part of Great Smoky Mountains National Park.

Wayne says his father usually kept at least two healthy horses at one time and rode them in turn, so that each got a thorough rest between rounds.

"This Tyson horse, when my father sold him, was taken out of Cades Cove," Wayne says. "Then he was later bought by another family that lived in Cades Cove and they brought Tyson back there.

"Those people told about Tyson stopping at all the mailboxes when they would try to ride him around the Cove."

Bill Cooper's bum steer

U.S. Geological Survey maps show Russell Field, on the main ridge of the Smokies above Cades Cove, to be 4,400 feet above sea level. Sam Sparks and family once had a farming and livestock grazing operation at Russell Field that may have been the highest year-round venture in the Smokies.

Longtime Knoxville garage and service station owner William C. Cooper knows a whole lot about farming at Russell Field. Beginning early in 1914, near the time of Bill's 14th birthday on Jan. 29, he

William C. Cooper was photographed as a young man working at Townsend sometime after his three-year livestock herding sojourn at Russell Field. Cooper and his wife Ena later lived on Woodlawn Pike in South Knoxville.

climbed the mountain and arrived in the midst of a deep snow to begin a stay of what would be almost three years, winter and summer.

Bill's mother, Emma Yearout Cooper, died when he was 8 years old and after that he lived awhile with his Uncle Cool Yearout and Cool's wife Alice. The Yearouts lived in Blount County at Cold Springs, where that creek flows into Ellejoy Creek on the north side of Chilhowee Mountain. Cool operated a grist mill there, and a cotton gin and a sawmill, all run by waterpower.

After several years away from his father, the late Thomas Cooper, the two became lonesome for each other, and finally Bill rejoined his father. They "batched," in Bill's language, wherever Tom found employment.

Then in January of 1914 Tom Cooper accepted a job of staying on the crest of the Smokies and looking after the Sparks family's cattle and sheep. Bill's brother Beecher, five years older, stayed with them awhile, but most of the time he was in school in Georgia.

Russell Field was one of the treeless meadows of the Smokies, but there wasn't much grazing there for cattle and sheep in winter. The summer hay crops were big ones, though, and the hay as it was harvested was stored in the mow of the big barn at the edge of the field. That may also have been the highest-altitude barn in the Smokies.

Bill says the Sparkses kept a horse-drawn mowing machine at the

Horse-drawn mowing machine similar to this one was probably dissembled and packed in on mule-back for use on Russell Field.

field, and he believes they may have gotten it to the top of the mountain by disassembling it and carrying it on the backs of pack animals. The most direct trail from the upper end of Cades Cove, up Anthony Creek and Anthony Ridge, was too rough for the machine to have been pulled there on its wheels, he says.

The cattle they were looking after were being raised for slaughter. But early in the stay there were 13 cows to be milked every day, after their suckling calves had finished.

The cabin in which the Coopers stayed was a one-room log house barely on the Tennessee side of the boundary with North Carolina. The state line runs along the crest for most of the length of the Great Smoky Mountains. Cooking was done with baker and lid in the wood-burning fireplace. The cabin's only heat was from the same fire.

Gregory's store was in Cades Cove at the foot of the trail and it was young Bill's duty to walk to the store at intervals and buy cornmeal for bread, and other grocery staples. He had a young steer he and his father had trained as a pack animal, and Bill would load two or three bushels of meal and other groceries on the steer's back at one time. A bushel of meal weighs more than 50 pounds. Cattle can be stubborn and unpredictable work animals, Bill says. "I remember one time that this steer balked. Laid down. Wouldn't get up at all. I got a handful of leaves and put on his tail and lit a match. Set the leaves afire. He got up from there then."

One-room pole cabin into which Bill Cooper and his father Thomas moved in 1914 had a sawmill boiler stack as part of its chimney. Logs to build the Russell Field cabin came from the woods a few yards away, as did the oak from which the roofing shingles were split. Wood was also plentiful for feeding the fireplace and a spring flowing from the mountain nearby was another convenience. The Coopers lived here summer and winter for most of three years.

(The late Roy Myers of Townsend grew up in the years when cattle were still being used as work animals. Roy was disappointed one day when his television set quit working at the height of an important football game. "It just quit like a steer in the road," he fumed.)

The Coopers had one horse on the mountain and they would sometimes ride it to come off into the Cove. They seldom dared the trip in winter because of ice and snow on the trail. In their second winter on the mountain, snow so deep it covered the pickets of the fence kept them there for three months without meal for making bread.

Root-hogs unwelcome on cattle range

This continues William C. Cooper's account of almost three years spent at Russell Field on the crest of the Smokies above Cades Cove. Bill and his father, Thomas Cooper, lived there in a herder's cabin summer and winter beginning early in 1914.

The Coopers planted corn, potatoes and turnips their first crop season at Russell Field. The potatoes became a landmark in Bill's life because of their great size, bigger than anything he has seen since. The turnips also did well.

They were planted in what farmers of his time called "new ground." It was a tract recently cleared from forest at McCampbell Gap, the first gap to the east in the direction of Spence Field. This was the first time the tract had been cultivated.

While the fertility of the new ground and the cool early season at 4,400 feet of altitude were favorable for potatoes and turnips, the short growing season at that level was against a good corn crop. "It didn't mature, and we fed it to the cattle green, while the corn was in the ear," Bill says.

The Coopers had as their main duties to look after Sam Sparks' cattle and sheep, all of which ranged at Russell Field and below there. Sam didn't turn any hogs loose on the mountain in the years the Coopers were there. But there were dozens and maybe hundreds of hogs owned by other families to worry them.

An owner put his earmark on each of his hogs before he turned it loose in the woods. An earmark was a notch of a certain shape cut into the ear, or maybe more than one notch. It was understood that all the pigs in the litter of a marked sow also belonged to the sow's owner.

Late in the season there were often unmarked pigs that strayed from the litter and ran wild in the woods. These unmarked strays, after they grew to full size, could be claimed legally by anybody who caught them or shot them. Strays were so abundant around Russell Field that the Coopers were seldom without fresh pork.

Fonz Cable, Cades Cove resident who was one of the more successful bear hunters in that section of the Smokies, would bring bear meat to the Coopers to swap for hog meat. Fonz did his bear hunting in the area of Spence Field and Thunderhead Mountain and would stop at the Cooper cabin on his way to and from.

It was the marked hogs that gave the Coopers trouble, Bill says. Most of their owners were sensitive to any harsh measures taken to

Sam Sparks' cattle and hay barn at Russell Field, on the main high ridge of the Smokies above Cades Cove. Mules in the foreground are grazing around rock outcrop which is abundant at Russell Field.

shoo them away from the potato patch. And if they weren't kept away they would root out the freshly-planted seed potatoes, and later in the season the growing potatoes.

More serious than their threat to the potato patch was what they could do to the lush mountaintop meadow of Russell Field. Before the chestnuts and acorns fell they plowed the sod for whatever edible morsels were there. "They'll just ruin a meadow, hogs will," Bill says.

Billy Gregory owned one sizeable lot of hogs that were giving trouble, and he was friendly with the Coopers. "Get some fine shot so you won't kill them, and shoot them with fine shot to scare them off," Billy suggested.

"I tried to be good to them (the hogs)," Bill recalls.

"I'd load the shotgun shells with meat skins, but the hogs wouldn't pay any attention. They'd only shake when I shot them with meat skins.

"So I did what Billy Gregory said, and I shot them with fine shot. They went off the mountain making wounded hog sounds. Billy wasn't real happy about it. He never could get those same hogs to come back to the mountain."

Bill says somebody else's hogs then started rooting in his potato patch and he went out there one Sunday with his shotgun, intending only to "burn their tails and scare them off."

"There was one hog must have weighed 150 pounds," Bill says. "I 'booshed' at them but they didn't run at all. The big one just 'booshed' back at me. I cut down on them with that shotgun. One shot hit one of them suckers in the eye and killed him. I didn't know what to do. There was a big bluff there and I dragged that son-of-a-gun out there and rolled him over that bluff. He laid there until he rotted. Nothing ever came of it."

The education of one country boy: reading, writing, and moonshining

This is the story of a Cades Cove boy who learned to make moonshine, but later found he had other skills that paid much better, and were legal and of benefit to society.

George W. Myers was born in the Chestnut Flats section at the west end of the cove. He was born Oct. 8, 1898, at the home of his grandfather, George Washington Powell, who was 58 years old that day. The boy was named for the grandfather.

About 1904, when he was 6 years old, George came to south Knox County to live with his divorced father, Henry Josiah Myers. While the father worked at Meade Quarry as a blacksmith, and for KS&E Railroad as a tool sharpener, the son attended the former Flenniken Elementary School, which then stood on Maryville Pike at the later site of Firehall 20.

Little George received his entire lifetime of public schooling, about 4 years, there at Flenniken while the family lived on Sims Road. He said in later years that he "paid in the end" for many violations of school discipline.

But on the foundation of less than four years in the classroom, George became an habitual reader and taught himself, from books, the mathematical calculations required in the machinist trade, several years away in his future.

When he was 12 years old George returned to the Smokies to live with his sisters and his mother, Harriet Powell Myers, and his apple-raising, brandy-distilling, game-hunting, sharpshooting, aging Civil War veteran grandfather Powell.

Old Powell's orchard of 2,000 apple and peach trees already had been productive for many years. Now he had somebody he hoped would perpetuate it, and he began to teach the grandson his knowledge of planting, grafting, pruning and picking. He taught him also how to make brandy in large quantity.

He taught him his great knowledge of beekeeping, learned over many years. Orchards, to bear fruit, must have bees at hand to pollinate the blossoms.

For some of the years young George was with him, old George had a federal license to run a distillery. The government kept a "storekeeper" there in Cades Cove to collect a tax on every keg of brandy distilled.

But there were several times through the years when all distilleries located in Tennessee became illegal. Once was when the Tennessee Legislature passed a short-lived law against them, and the final time, for Powell, was when national prohibition arrived as the 18th Amendment to the U.S. Constitution, in January 1919.

With tons of apples and peaches on hand, and not much else to do with them, Powell is known to have made brandy illegally. And the fact that he was now a moonshiner was probably not as big a surprise to his neighbors as was his earlier decision to get a federal license.

Old Powell preferred a legal market for his apples when he could find one. His grandson and others who worked for him made many horse-and-wagon trips out of the cove, across Cades Cove Mountain and Rich Mountain, to peddle apples in Maryville and the nearby growing town of Alcoa where the Aluminum Company of America was building.

Brandy, especially that which was government-stamped, went out in charred oak kegs, one keg strapped to each side of a horse's or mule's pack saddle. Sometimes it was hauled in wagons and sometimes on farm sleds.

Feist welcomed into menagerie

*John McCaulley was driving his mules home from
Maryville one day when he noticed a friendly little pup
running beside the wagon, and back and forth under it.
John stopped to try to run her back in the direction of town.
He guessed she belonged to somebody who lived close to
the road. But the dog, a short-haired feist, wouldn't be
chased away, and was still with him a mile or more up the
road. John finally lifted her into the wagon for the rest of
the ride home, past Dry Valley and across Rich
Mountain into Cades Cove.*

"That was old Maude," John Earl McCaulley says. "I can remember her as a little pup, and we kept her until she was old. She was a good squirrel dog. She'd tree squirrels, but not coons."

The McCaulley menagerie of animals and pets also included milk cows, one or more brood sows, a white burro, the mules already mentioned, and a pack of coondogs whose number varied by the season.

John bought the first of his coonhounds, a female Plott, out of North Carolina and raised pups from her. The coondogs doubled for hunting bear, and in time the McCaulleys were raising hunting dogs, training them and selling them. They always had one or more hounds for the mountain hunting trips they guided.

The mules, a horse mule named Frank and a mare mule named Hattie, lived a long time and helped the McCaulleys earn a living for most of it.

"Dad worked at Calderwood in 1916. I was too young to remember it, but George Tipton told me about it later," John Earl says. "George was a good size boy, and he had gone to Calderwood to get a job.

"He said John McCaulley was working there with the mules and a slip (dirt moving pan). They were putting the last half-mile of railroad in." (That was the railroad to Calderwood, the Aluminum Company of America's base camp then for the series of hydroelectric dams it was beginning to build on Little Tennessee River.)

John Earl remembers plowing with Frank in 1929. That was 13 years after the Calderwood job, and Frank was not a colt at Calderwood. "Dad sold old Frank to Willie Effler up in the '30s, and Frank must have been 30 years old then – maybe older," John Earl says. The mules were McCaulley's pack animals when he was guiding groups of hikers, campers and hunters to Gregory Bald and Spence Field. First he'd take the mules and a wagon to the Little River Railroad station that was then called Riverside. It was close to where Wilson's Restaurant later stood, at the lower end of Townsend.

He'd pick up the tents, blankets, extra clothing and food supplies the campers had brought. He'd haul that into Cades Cove in the wagon, and transfer it to the backs of the mules for the long climb to the bald.

John Earl made some of the pack trips before he was in his teens. He carried cattle salt to George Potter's herd cabin below Gregory Bald on the Tennessee side.

"I'd saddle the little mules of a morning, load them with salt, take it to the cabin. If the men weren't there I'd just unload it. Then I'd throw the stirrups up over the saddles and turn the mules loose. And I'd beat them home."

The McCaulleys also had a burro that was smaller than the mare mule. "We never did have a name for the burro, except that we'd call it the little burro. We'd load it almost as heavy as we'd load the mules," John Earl says.

The burro and the mare mule became close friends, almost in a human way. They'd jump the rail fence at the place on Post Branch, and head for the gant lot east of Gregory Bald, seven miles away.

"When they'd be gone, we almost knew we'd find them at the gant lot," John Earl says. It was as if they enjoyed, in a way, a visit to the top of the Great Smoky Mountains.

But the last time they ran away from home they didn't return, and the McCaulleys never did see them again. "We heard they were shot, up there next to the gant lot," John Earl says. "We never did find even their carcasses."

Baked 'coon for Thanksgiving

John McCaulley's wider fame was as a hunter of wild turkey, but he was also a daylight 'coon stalker of local renown. Daughter Anna Lee Coulter remembered baked 'coon as a frequent menu item through late fall and winter.

Except for pork in abundance, wild meat was the main fare on the McCaulley table in their years in the Forge Creek wilderness at the edge of Cades Cove. They lived there from 1908 through 1936 when they moved out to make way for the new Great Smoky Mountains National Park.

Maymie McCaulley Tipton said her mother, Rutha, stepped aside when 'coon was to be cooked, and that her father did it all for the special meal. John McCaulley had an uncommonly large Dutch oven, or baker and lid, bought at one of the Maryville hardware stores. He'd bake the 'coon in that, but first he'd parboil it in water seasoned with a pod of hot pepper, Maymie said.

He'd then transfer the meat to his oven, as he called it, and he'd set the oven in hot coals in the fireplace. He'd season the meat with lots of black pepper and ring it with sweet potatoes. He'd put on the rimmed lid and cover it with more hot coals. Maymie and her brother John Earl McCaulley remembered that baked 'coon was their Thanksgiving meal often enough to be traditional.

"People didn't celebrate it (Thanksgiving) like they do now, but a 'coon would be tender and marbled with fat from the fall chestnut crop, and most of us looked forward to that meal," John Earl said. There were as many as 10 McCaulleys, parents and children, at the table sometimes, and maybe other company. John and his older sons, Millard and John Earl, would prepare for that by bringing home more than one 'coon.

The sale of raccoon pelts was one of John McCaulley's chief livelihoods. John Earl said there was a period when a prime coonskin brought $9, the price ranging down to $4 for lesser pelts. The hides would be tacked to the side of the house to dry.

Jerry Hearon, from Happy Valley below Cades Cove, would walk to the cove at intervals and stay two or three days at the Burchfield store on Forge Creek, two miles below the McCaulley home. The word would be passed that Jerry was there and people who had furs to sell would take them to the store. Jerry would pay cash and carry his cargo home threaded on a stick balanced on his shoulder. McCaulley did well enough as a coonhunter that he quit an industrial job at least once to return to the cove and hunt that winter.

The baked 'coon for Thanksgiving was a sample of the forever-something-different in the lives of the McCaulleys. Anna Lee said their Easter meal was baked wild turkey. "I like to think back on times like that," Maymie said.

Hemlock a haven for wild turkey

*Three wild turkey hunters of renown, from the western end
of the Great Smoky Mountains in Tennessee, were John
McCaulley from Cades Cove and the brothers Tom and
Jerry Hearon from Happy Valley. A younger Hearon
brother, Dave, was about as skillful but not as well known.*

Freeland Godfrey could make a gobbling sound with his throat,
as natural as a tom turkey's. John McCaulley was his hunting teacher
and frequent companion, and named one of his sons for Godfrey. The
son, Freeland, born in 1917 in the family's original log house in Post
Branch Hollow, later lived at Walland.

Commodore "Commie" Tipton was a rifle sharpshooter who also
learned to stalk the wild turkey. He died in 1984, the youngest and
last survivor of those mentioned. There may have been others. It is
probable that there were hunters whose unwritten legends died with
them, or with the passing of those who knew them.

Some hunters fed their families on wild meat. And some of the
families wished that their providers would spend more time at agri-
culture, at growing corn and garden vegetables and at raising domestic livestock – chickens, hogs, cattle.

Roy M. Myers said that some of the old hunters with big families,
when they had a choice, would kill the biggest, oldest turkey or 'coon
that they had a shot at. That was because they could take more meat
home in one heavy carcass that was still easier to carry than several
smaller, more tender specimens.

Even a resilient stomach might rebel at constant fare of squirrel,
groundhog, possum and tough old tom turkey that had to be stewed
a long time before it could be chewed. Anna Effler Maples recalled
how she dreaded to see her father, Will Effler, come home to Dry
Valley with such a bird.

But young, tender wild turkey was another eating experience.

73

S. Earle Crawford, retired Maryville dentist, recalled how welcome it was on one of his Gregory Bald trips with John McCaulley in the early 1920s.

John had killed, dressed and cooked a groundhog in the fireplace coals of the herder's cabin near the Gant Lot. Then along came two North Carolina boys who had killed two young turkey hens, and John cooked those, too.

The groundhog, an elderly specimen, was on the slab table first. Earle was trying to eat some of it, but not able to look pleased about it. "That groundhog was really tough," Earle said reminiscing in 1984. "They passed the turkey, and after I tasted that turkey, I looked to the open window, and pitched Mr. Groundhog out the window. "You can't imagine how young, wild turkey tasted – a most delicate flavor!"

John Earl McCaulley said his father's reputation as foremost turkey hunter grew partly from his living so close to the wild bird's main range. His home off Forge Creek was at the foot of the mountain slope that had the greatest turkey population.

In John McCaulley's day, before the blight killed the American chestnut that was one of the most abundant tree species of the Smokies, the turkey prospered on the bountiful fall nut crop.

Chestnut trees grew to the main ridge of the Smokies, even to the shoulder of the higher bald mountains, Thunderhead, Gregory Bald and Parsons Bald. It was on the ridge, or under it on the Tennessee side of the boundary, that McCaulley and the others did most of their hunting.

In bad weather the turkey flocks would roost in the hemlock stands of the hollows under the main ridge, John Earl said. The hemlock, often called "spruce pine" by people who grew up in the Smokies, is there today, to be seen by those who will walk to it.

It is so dense in places that scant light penetrates, and the turkey was sheltered there from snow, rain and sleet. They would roost there for days, John Earl said.

The Park Service stopped all hunting when it moved in, and John McCaulley was soon busy at other things—building roads with the CCC, working for the Park Service.

December 13, 1894

Indian ancestry never confirmed

John McCaulley believed that one of his near ancestors was Cherokee Indian. His oldest daughter, Maymie Tipton of Townsend, said he discussed it with his family but died without being able to confirm who the Indian ancestor was.

John was the last of several children of James McCaulley and Unity Elizabeth Caldwell. He spent more time with his dad than did

John McCaulley's father, Jim McCaulley

most of the older children. They traipsed a wide range of the Smokies together, hunting and trapping bear on Defeat Ridge and Thunderhead, tending their livestock in the mountains above Cades Cove.

The father taught the son the blacksmith skills he had learned as a Union cavalry soldier in the Civil War. He taught young John how to survive in the woods, how to cook wild game without pans or other utensils, how to build a mountain camper's lean-to in a few minutes.

He taught his youngest son how to prepare the dead for burial, and how to make a coffin from raw lumber. The father, to his death in 1906, and then the son, acted as undertakers to dozens of Cades Cove residents who died in their time.

But James McCaulley didn't talk much about his own, or his wife's, origins. Their descendants know now that he was born in 1832, probably in Tennessee, and that his wife Unity was born in 1841, probably in North Carolina. They know that they were born in a time of uncertainty for people of Cherokee, or even of mixed, ancestry. The forced removal of the tribe from lands in the Southeast began when James was a child. The exodus to lands west of the Mississippi had ended by the time Unity was born in 1841.

Some families of mixed white and Indian ancestry were able to escape the removal by living in secluded places and by not calling

Patricia "Trish" McCaulley Abbott says she pointed a simple box camera at her grand-parents, John and Rutha McCaulley for this snapshot in the fall of 1959. John looked up from his whittling when she called, and Rutha smiled because she doubted there was film in the camera. Trish was 14 then, and in earlier, childhood years had "fooled" her grandmother with an empty camera.

attention to themselves. They learned not to talk about themselves, and not talking became a habit that lasted long past the time when it became safe again to be Indian and live in the Smokies.

Maycle McCaulley Yearout, of Maryville, believes her grandfather, John McCaulley, enjoyed the thought that he might be part-Chero-kee, however small or large a fraction of his ancestry it was. "I believe he 'wanted' to be Indian," Maycle says.

John often traveled to Cherokee, N.C., in his final years, after a road was built across the Smokies. He became a close friend to Willie Owl, Cherokee resident, and Willie conducted his funeral when John McCaulley died in 1961. When Willie Owl died in 1984, a contingent of McCaulleys crossed the mountain to be at his Indian-Christian funeral.

John Earl McCaulley recalled a hunting trip in which he thought he would freeze to death while his father, John, talked most of the night and appeared to be very comfortable.

It was a winter hunt for deer in an area west of Cades Cove and west of Hannah Mountain. With them were some of the other ardent hunters of the Abrams Creek valley, Harve Whitehead and the brothers Tom and Jerry Hearon among them.

They were in a lean-to that one of them, maybe John McCaulley, had built in better weather. He would put up such a shelter, build it sturdy and roof it with chestnut bark, with the thought that it would last a year or more, and that he would come back to it sometime.

Having shelters at convenient places is what allowed John McCaulley to tramp the Smokies without a bed roll. Usually the open

McCaulley family outing on Gregory Bald, in the 1920s, included (from left) daughter Icele; mother Rutha; son Freeland riding Frank the mule; friend Oral Brandon, from Mascot; his son Richard, only his hat showing, on the burro; Nell (Mrs.) Brandon; John Earl McCaulley on Hattie the mule; Anna Lee McCaulley next to her father, John. The youngest child, J.C., was yet to be born.

end of the lean-to would face a boulder, or pile of rock, and the rock would reflect the heat of a fire back into the shelter.

It was so cold, that night under Hannah Mountain, that it forced the moisture out of the ground in inverted icicles. But the great hunters laughed the night away as they regaled one another with memories of past adventures. "Except me. I couldn't sleep for the cold, and for them talking all night," John Earl said.

WOMEN PLAYED BACKGROUND ROLE 4

Becky Cable, mountain woman

Rebecca "Becky" Cable was a Cades Cove resident whose name is on some of the historical markers put up by the National Park Service. She never did marry, but she was as active a farmer as some of her successful men neighbors.

Several people interviewed for these pages knew Becky personally and well. They all confirm that she had her own farming and grazing tract in what was known locally as "Becky's Sugar Cove," or "Cable Sugar Cove," in a high hollow that is a branch of Mill Creek

Henry Rankin Duncan, professor of animal husbandry at University of Tennessee, is regarded as an authority on the lay of local mountains, the Smokies and the Chilhowees which flank the Smokies to the north and

Becky Cable

west. "Prof" Duncan's friends have tagged him the "Sage of the Chilhowees." He's very much at home in the Cove, though and he has known many of its former and present inhabitants down through the years.

Duncan remarked that most of the Cove folk whose memories

79

have lasted were men. That's because the women of the Cove stayed in the background. However much they loved their families and were loved by them in return, usually they were in the background with relation to the world beyond the mountains which wall the Cove.

An exceptional Cove woman in many ways was Becky Cable. She did a man's work for all but the first and last few of her 96 years. Duncan said he doubts she ever wasted a waking moment. As a girl, she tramped the ridges barefooted driving her cattle to and from high range. She could swing an axe, pull a saw, drive a team, and probably could have conquered a bear if the need arose.

There was another side to Becky. She could knit and weave garments and coverlets with a feminine touch of design. And her work-

Becky Cable sheared her sheep, spun yarn, dyed it with homemade vegetable dyes and wove the coverlet displayed by Elsie Morrell and Mary Deaderick Duncan to a 1955 tour group.

manship was of finest quality.

Professor Duncan recalled that Becky knitted socks at 50 cents per pair for as many customers as would come to her. One time the Prof's father ordered a pair and Becky sent them to him by mail.

The elder Duncan had to send them back for "alteration." They were too short for his larger-than-average feet.

But not more than a few days elapsed before the socks came back to Duncan. This time they fit, for Becky had knitted in an "extension" which made them now large enough.

Becky raised sheep. She did the shearing. She carded the wool. And it was Becky who on a spinning wheel spun the wool fibers into yarn. She prepared vegetable dyes. She dyed the wool yarn. On a handloom she wove the yarn into coverlets.

The late John McCaulley was born in Cades Cove in 1880 when Becky was already 36 years old. As a young man and as an aging man he knew her, and this is some of what McCaulley had to say about Becky Cable, before his own death in 1961.

Becky Cable with her spinning wheel on the porch of her home. Boy in the foreground is Virgil Tipton.

"She was a fine woman. Intelligent woman. Ain't no question about that. And she went barefoot the most of the time. I've seen her when she ranged her own cattle in the mountains. She'd hang her shoes on her arm of a morning and she'd come back that night with them still hanging on her arm – tramping all day.

"Becky never did get married. Never in the world."

"She told me one day she was going around there from the Sugar Cove to what we called the Rough Ridge. And it was awful rough through there. And said she was going the way a big spruce pine had blown down. Made her a pretty open route.

"Said she stepped on something that was awful cold. And her barefooted. And she just stepped on off and looked back and said it was a big rattlesnake coiled up. She'd stepped on him and then stepped off of him. She says 'old feller, you was good to me, I'll be good to you. I'll not kill you. I'll just go on'."

Becky had the first iron pitchfork her family owned. Her father John P. Cable bought it in Carter County, their original home, when she was a small girl. Before he brought the metal pitchfork home the family had used forked sticks to put up their hay crops, McCaulley said. Becky worked in the hayfields and the cornfields like a man, and she knew the value of having proper tools.

They took special care of that pitchfork. McCaulley said that in Becky Cable's day intelligent people were careful with the tools they owned for farming and making a living. Axes, shovels, mattocks, hoes and pitchforks were

> *"She'd take her shoes of a morning and she'd hang them on her arm."*

sometimes in shorter supply on a big farm than they are with many a backyard gardener today.

McCaulley and family lived in a hollow not far from where Becky Cable lived. He worked with her and for her many times through the years. He esteemed her friendship. One day as he was passing her home she called him inside.

"I've got a present that I want to give you," Becky began. "You've made all of our coffins and I've knit you a pair of wool socks that'll come up to your knees. They'll keep your feet warm this winter and I'm going to make you a present of them," Becky told McCaulley.

Rebecca Cable lived so long and befriended so many that it was inevitable she be called Aunt Becky by most of her Cades Cove neighbors. Because of her long, productive life she has become perhaps the most publicized of all women who lived in Cades Cove before the Great Smoky Mountains National Park was created.

She in fact was an aunt by family to a number of people, including William M. "Bill" Post, a great-nephew living near Maryville in our final weeks of putting this book together.

While looking into the mystery of who put the new tombstone on Becky's grave, we learned Bill had done it.

The original stone had been shattered and left lying at the gravesite by persons known perhaps only to themselves. W. Lee Tipton, a former neighbor to Becky, spoke of the stone as Becky's *tomb rock* and was among those who regarded its destruction as a personal loss.

Bill's father was John C. Post, a carpenter who forever enjoyed going back to the Cove after he moved out in 1905. John was given the job of dismantling the former Laurel Springs School in Chestnut Flats and rebuilding it on what is now Cable Cemetery.

Lifelong friendship began in mountain fog

August 1914, on a rainy weekend in Cades Cove, S. Earle Crawford and five friends came to Becky Cable's door. The home, since moved a short distance from its old location, is preserved today in the Cable Mill complex at the lower end of the cove.

Earle and companions told Becky that they intended to walk to Gregory Bald, a climb of another nine miles or more.

It was too foggy on the mountain for them to be starting up there that late in the day, Becky warned. "You come in here and I'll fix you something to eat," she said.

"She didn't know us from Adam. She took us in. Gave us our supper. Put us in feather beds so deep we didn't need any covers. Next morning she fed us breakfast. She charged us 50 cents each — that was for everything," Earle recalled.

Hikers at the herder's cabin below the gant lot were (left to right) Robert Clemens, S. Earle Crawford, Edwin Ellis, Elmer Brown, Raymond Smith and Henry Callaway, all of Maryville. Their ages were 18 to 24. Crawford says he made the picture by weighting the camera under a rock and pulling a string to trip the shutter.

Next morning was still very foggy. "You boys are away from home. You're in my care now. I don't want you to go to the mountain in that fog," Aunt Becky told them. She sent for a neighbor, John McCaulley, to ask John to be their guide.

It was the first time any of the six had met McCaulley. For Earle Crawford, it would become a friendship that would endure from that day on.

Earle would be leaving Maryville in a month to enroll in a school of dentistry in Kansas City. He would finish at Vanderbilt and be tempted to return to practice dentistry in Missouri. But vacation visits to Cades Cove with John McCaulley and his wife Rutha had expanded his love and knowledge of the Great Smoky Mountains.

John McCaulley, 34 years old, was photographed in 1914 on Gregory Bald by S. Earle Crawford. The hike was their first meeting, and began a friendship that lasted to McCaulley's death in 1961.

He came back to Maryville to begin a career as a dentist. "John McCaulley had a big impact on my life. He was one of the most versatile men I knew. He taught me patience. He got me into beekeeping," Earle said.

McCaulley had stands of tame, "civilized" bees, but also had colonies of a wild, testy, black bee. He had a big bee yard and built a protective shed over it below his home in a hollow that is a branch of Forge Creek.

To show Earle how safely he could handle his gentler bees, John went into one of the hives. "Now don't breathe on them," he cautioned Earle. "Bees don't like the odor of human breath."

From a washpan on the porch, or from a cold mountain stream, John McCaulley impressed Earle with the thoroughness of his morning scrub of hands, arms, face and neck. "He was meticulously clean.

He was a good cook. He could prepare a complete meal. "There was love in the McCaulley home, between John and his wife Rutha, and all of their children. You could see it at every turn," Earle said.

McCaulley could track bear, call wild turkeys, play a banjo, preach a sermon, and sing bass to the delight of fellow members of the Cades Cove Missionary Baptist Church.

He made wooden coffins, without charge and without accepting payment, for many of the people who died in Cades Cove over a period of 35 years. That was from his early manhood to 1936, the year he left the cove after it was made part of the Great Smoky Mountains National Park.

One of his older children, John Earl McCaulley, says of him:

"He was a character of a man. He'd always draw a crowd, wherever he was and went to talking. They'd gather around and listen, you know. He was a great talker."

Brass handles for Becky's coffin

*John McCaulley's father, James, moved to Cades Cove
after Civil War service in the Union Army and in his time
may have been the Cove's busiest maker of coffins. The son
helped the father and continued the service after the
father's death. But John McCaulley was never the Cove's
only coffin maker, his daughter, Maymie Tipton, said.
She named Witt Shields and Manuel Ledbetter, and said
there may have been others with the woodworking
skills and the willingness.*

Witt Shields lived near the middle of the cove and had a building in which he kept the tools and lumber for making coffins. The neighbors called his little building the coffin shop. Witt died in 1919, and the years immediately following may have been John McCaulley's busiest. Maymie as a young girl sometimes helped him. She said he shaped all his coffins the old, traditional way, narrow at the feet and head, and wide at the shoulders. The corpse was measured, and the casket was built to fit the corpse.

McCaulley sometimes called it a casket and sometimes called it a coffin. The two long sides of the coffin were each built of one wide board. Walnut, chestnut, cherry, white pine, cedar and poplar were used. McCaulley liked walnut for the natural beauty of the wood and its pleasant aroma. The boards had to be bent, and that's where Maymie helped her father the most.

He would lay the boards flat and saw almost through each one in two places. The sawed places would make the board easier to bend. To keep the board from breaking at the sawed place, Maymie would pour steaming water on it to soften it. McCaulley would then fasten the sideboards to the bottom, using screws or nails. Screws increased the likelihood that the coffin would keep its shape. And the use of screws to fasten the lid was more insurance that the box would remain intact during a rough wagon ride to the cemetery and while being lowered into the grave.

Maymie said her father made coffins outdoors when the weather allowed. Sometimes he would take his hand tools, saw, plane, square, hammer, etc., to the home of a neighbor who lived closer to the deceased. The availability of wide boards would also determine where it would be made. It was a custom in Cades Cove that when choice lumber was being produced at local sawmills, some of it would be stored, perhaps in a barn loft, until it was needed for making a coffin.

In a 1960 interview, a year before his death at age 81, McCaulley said that nobody in his experience had ever been asked to pay for coffin lumber. He said also that he had never taken money for making coffins "in all the days of my life."

> "You've made all of our coffins, and I've knit you a pair of wool socks that'll come up to your knees."

He did say that his neighbor, Becky Cable, called him into the house one day and told him she had knitted him a pair of wool socks "that'll come up to your knee and keep your feet warm this winter." She was giving him the socks, she said, "because you've made all of our coffins."

When Becky Cable was getting along in years she gradually cut down on the amount of work she would try unassisted. Her last team of horses and wagon she sold to John McCauley.

As Becky sold that last team, she must have thought her life was drawing to a close. She told John she wanted him to have her a coffin made. That was part of her "price" for the team. John said he would make the coffin.

McCaulley had already moved his family out of Cades Cove when word came to him that Aunt Becky was ailing. McCaulley at the time was doing work on the road to Happy Valley with a group of CCC enrollees.

When he heard of Becky's illness he took two men down the mountain to a sawmill in Happy Valley. He bought some of the widest, cleanest yellow poplar boards as lumber for her coffin. He tried to find walnut, but it had become scarce. He hauled the boards by truck to his home near Hubbard, between Walland and Maryville. He made the coffin in his shop there. McCaulley then hauled it to Cades Cove in his pickup truck, and she was buried in it in the Cable Cemetery.

But Becky recovered from that illness. The coffin stayed in his workshop at the family's new home on Piney Level Road east of Maryville, north of Chilhowee Mountain. Finally, when she did die on Dec. 19, 1940, McCaulley hauled the coffin to Cades Cove and she was buried there in it. She was a few days more than 96 years old.

Becky's coffin was the last one John McCaulley made.

John Earl McCaulley said his father gave the coffin a decorative and useful feature inspired by the factory-made caskets in which most burials were now being made.

For Becky, and for the first time, he put six brass carrying handles on the box.

John Rice Irwin shows one of the coffins on display in his Museum of Appalachia. This one, for a child, is in the style in which McCaulley and others made coffins for the families of Cades Cove — wide at the shoulders and narrow at each end. The cover stands partially hidden beside the coffin.

Lonely life of the hunter's wife

The Smoky Mountain home that John McCaulley yearned to move back to in his final years may have been less than a paradise for his wife, Rutha Myers McCaulley.

It was a home without close neighbors. It stood in a hollow so deep that the sun entered late and left early. There was no electricity, no telephone, and the nearest store, Jane Burchfield's general store, was two miles down Forge Creek. The wide, flat, open expanses of the lower end of Cades Cove were yet a half-mile farther.

John Earl McCaulley says his parents bought the 75 acres in Post Branch Hollow for $2 an acre, for a total of $150. They moved there in October 1908 into a log house already standing, low in the hollow beside a spring and beside the creek. They bought it from the family of Manuel Ledbetter on a personal note, with no bank or other lending agency involved.

"They (the Ledbetters) were easy with my dad in how he could pay for it. He was working at a sawmill then for 50 cents a day. He paid a little along, whenever he could. And maybe he got to making more money soon after that," John Earl says.

At the same time they bought the farm, the McCaulleys bought a horse for $50 from the John Hitch family, also on personal credit. The Hitches were big-scale farmers outside the Cove, in Blount County north of Chilhowee Mountain. The McCaulleys, John and some of his brothers, may have tended the Hitch cattle on summer range on and near Gregory Bald. John's and Rutha's new home was a few yards up Post Branch from the cattle drovers' main trail from Cades Cove to Gregory Bald.

The horse they bought would serve for plowing, for dragging firewood down from the steep slopes above them, or for hauling a bear carcass home from a hunt on Thunderhead Mountain. The same horse saddled was their ride to Cable Mill, two miles down Forge

Creek to Mill Creek, to have their corn ground into meal.

Most of the new McCaulley farm was too steep for growing corn. "We raised a little corn, but most of the time we bought corn for cornmeal, or to feed our livestock," John Earl says.

"Or sometimes we rented better corn land down in the Cove. We rented land from Aunt Becky Cable once. We had to buy hay, too. We had no land to make hay. We had good truck (garden) patches. We raised potatoes, cabbage, beans, stuff like that.

"There was a big family of us and we lived, I think, pretty good. We canned lots in the summer. She (mother Rutha) was a healthy woman. We all worked hard."

John Earl says most of his mother's complaints were about the loneliness and worry of her life in a secluded mountain hollow when her children were small.

Her husband, in his words, was a "mountain man" who was gone from home for days sometimes, hunting bear, or raccoon or wild turkey, or guiding hunters and campers. Or he might be gone for weeks herding livestock.

These are John McCaulley's own words in 1960, a year before his death at the age of 81:

"I've spent half of my life on Smoky Mountain. Laid out just wherever night came on me. Kindled me up a fire. Just laid down there and

**Drawing of the McCaulley home in Post Branch Hollow was
by Freeland, one of four McCaulley sons.**

went to sleep. Got up next morning and went on about my business."

John Earl says, though, that when his father was at home he would usually share in whatever labor was at hand. He would help with the cooking, help with the gardening, help with the firewood.

Another son, Freeland McCaulley, has a memory of his father sitting by the fire playing his homemade banjo and singing while Rutha fixed breakfast. Sometimes she would join him in singing as she worked.

It was their talent for music and their enjoyment of it that brought them together and led to their marriage in 1901. He would sing as he walked or rode a mule down Forge Creek, and his neighbors would halt their work to listen as his deep voice carried across the bottoms. "Bringing in the Sheaves" was his favorite.

July 2, 1986

Frances Brown brought home the gravy

Working her way through high school was less than satisfying
for Frances Whitehead from Cades Cove.

"It was a hard thing to do, to go to school in town and do house-work for somebody for room and board. While you were in class, they'd be thinking up chores for you to do. You had to forget about homework. I got disgusted with it and quit.

"After that I worked in an underwear factory in Knoxville for $12 a week. Then I came home (to Cades Cove) and did a lot of fishing, and listened to the quails whistle. I helped my mother hoe the garden. I didn't like being penned up in town."

She is now Frances Brown, wife of Carl Brown. They have six children, all grown and gone. The Browns live at Almond, N.C., at the upper end of Fontana Lake. The home is one of several Carl has built with his hands and ingenuity in their 63 years of marriage.

Frances was youngest of 11 children of Mary Jane Gregory and Taylor Whitehead. Mary Jane was a granddaughter of Russell Gregory, who was murdered by Civil War bushwhackers with no loyalty to either cause, Union or Confederate.

Frances' brother, Russell Whitehead, 98 years old and a resident of Care Inn at Maryville, says Gregory was killed demanding payment for cattle the guerrillas had taken in a Cades Cove raid. Gregory Bald was named for him.

Some of the old martyr's stand-up-to-people stubbornness shows in these two great-grandchildren, and Russ has yet another tribute (for his baby sister and her husband). It's about their resourcefulness.

"Put Carl and Frances on a flat rock somewhere and they'd still find a way to raise plenty to eat," Russ says.

Frances says that when she goes back to Forge Creek, to where the Whitehead home stood at the junction of Parsons Branch Road, "it's as if time had dissolved between now and then. Tom Wolfe didn't know. You do go home – absolutely go home," she says.

(Thomas Wolfe's last novel, *You Can't Go Home Again,* was published in 1940, two years after his death at the age of 38. The story was an account of the resentment his first novel, *Look Homeward Angel,* met in his hometown of Asheville, North Carolina. Little more than the names of people and places were disguised in the novels. If Wolfe had written more kindly of Asheville, or not at all, he might have gone home again and been welcome. But would we remember him today?)

Back to Frances:

"And down at old Cable mill, I was a big rough tomboy. All the older kids got jobs and left home. There was just me to help dad.

"Dad was getting old and I was big and strong by then and enjoyed helping him. I worked outside a lot. I could do about anything – pull a saw or whatever was to be done.

"I drove old Marg and Mandy (sorrel mares) out of Tipton Sugar Cove with 50 bushel of apples in a wagon.

"It was a lucky thing for me I was developed that way, for I've had a lot of it to do. I had a lifetime of it in front of me after I married this woodsman (Carl Brown).

"I've hunted lots. Sometimes it was the difference between gravy and no gravy the next morning. I was on the ways and means committee a long time ago."

July 8, 1982

Daughters helped make bricks for chimney

Russell "Rusty" Whitehead was born 94 years ago in Cades Cove and remembers nearly 90 years of it. His father was Taylor Whitehead and his mother was Mary Jane Gregory, granddaughter of the Russell Gregory who gave his name to Gregory Bald.

The Whiteheads and their 10 children lived on Forge Creek toward Gregory Bald from the lower end of Cades Cove. The farm where they lived was called the Post place, and in more recent years the Willie Myers place. The hollows are deep in that section of Forge Creek. The giant poplar that stood until recent years on the walking trail to Gregory Bald was close to their home.

The family of Rutha and John McCaulley, the Cades Cove coffin maker and wild turkey hunter of renown, lived in a hollow off Forge Creek near where the Whiteheads lived. The families were friends. Another neighbor was Henry Whitehead and family who lived a short distance down Forge Creek in a home that is preserved today by Great Smoky Mountains National Park.

Russell says his father and Henry Whitehead were second cousins. "My dad was partly raised at Six Mile (north of Chilhowee Mountain in Blount County), and Uncle Henry was raised close to there, up about Old Piney.

"They both knowed a lot of them old settlers out in there – the Potters and Kellers. They had lots to talk about. He liked to come to our house when we lived close to him there in Cades Cove," Russell says. These are some of Russell Whitehead's memories of Henry Whitehead and family:

"Occasionally people would kill a sheep for the mutton. They'd take the hide off and preserve it with the wool on. Uncle Henry had such a sheep hide. He'd spread it on the front porch and lie on it to rest.

95

"Uncle Henry would work of a morning while it was cool. Then he laid up through the heat of the day on that sheep hide, and he'd work some more of an evening.

"I stayed there one night, in cool weather, and he laid on it in front of the fire. He turned a straight chair down and used it for a back rest. He'd lay there in front of the fire on his sheep hide and chew his tobacco and spit in the ashes.

"He was a great old fellow. There were no other men about his

Henry Whitehead and his three daughters dug the clay and molded and fired the brick for the nearest chimney of this home which stands today on Forge Creek. The home has been restored by the National Park Service, the chimney still as it was when Henry spread a sheepskin to warm himself in front of it.

house to talk to. He had three daughters and his wife, and he was the only male there was in the family."

Henry's first wife was Sarah Margaret Boring. They had three young daughters when Sarah Margaret died. The father and daughters then moved from Old Piney to Cades Cove, where Henry married Tilda Shields.

Russell says Henry and the daughters molded and fired the brick for the chimney of the new home they built on Forge Creek, the home that is open to the public and is maintained by the National Park Service.

Clay for the brick came from one of the deep, nearby hollows that the family called the Brick Kiln Hollow. The girls pressed the clay into homemade wooden molds and then "burnt" or baked the bricks in a wood fire.

"They got old Uncle Jim McCaulley (John McCaulley's father) to build the chimney. Jim was a rock mason mostly, but he did a good job building that chimney," Russell says.

"They had the best little fireplace in that house. It would warm that little house up good as you wanted it. Didn't smoke a bit. Had a good draft to it. Pull that smoke up there and burn your wood all up.

"Uncle Henry and his family made a good living there. They all worked like men. They made lots of garden vegetables and raised a few hogs and a few cattle. Kept some milk cows.

"He'd have only four or five head of beef cattle at a time. He'd take them up to Ekaneetlee Gap, right above his place, and look after them himself so he wouldn't have to pay a herd bill. Ran his hogs up there, too."

Russell says Henry's oldest daughter, Jane, married Russell Burchfield. His second daughter, Nancy Ann, married John W. Oliver. The youngest, Susan, married Walter Gregory.

Cove married years cherished as a love affair too brief

On the very cold morning of January 21, 1941, Polly Smith was counting the curves on the old mountain road between Cades Cove and Townsend.

"It has 219 curves – most of the worst ones on the Cades Cove side of the mountain," Polly would recall.

"Try to hold off just a little while longer," Clyde Smith pleaded with his wife every few minutes.

Polly remembered laughing at her husband and saying, "Clyde, I can't hold back. When this baby's ready to be born, it'll be born."

The child was given the name of Judy. She was born in the right front seat of the Smiths' 1936 model Chevrolet sedan, somewhere near the top of the climb out of the Cove, in the flat section called Eldorado between Cades Cove Mountain and Rich Mountain.

"Should I stop the car or keep going?" Clyde asked Polly after the baby was born.

"Keep going. But there's no hurry now," Polly said.

Clyde did ease back on the gas pedal. The gravel road was icy, and in the best of weather it was not designed for speed. It was the only motor road in and out of Cades Cove before today's paved highway, up Laurel Creek and through Crib Gap, was completed early in the 1950s.

Their destination the morning in 1941 was the Fort Craig Hospital that then served Maryville. There the mother and daughter were both found to he healthy, although baby Judy had made almost no sound the entire automobile trip. She is still Judy Smith, married to Stan Smith, and they live in Virginia Beach, Va.

Clyde and Polly met while she lived in Chattanooga and he was a surveyor and timber cruiser for Tennessee Valley Authority, in preparation for the building of nearby Chickamauga Dam and TVA installations in north Alabama.

He came to work for Great Smoky Mountains National Park in January of 1938, as first ranger assigned to live in and watch over Cades Cove. Clyde and Polly were married in May of 1938, and a farm home near the entrance to the CCC camp was their first. They soon moved into another farm home on Tater Branch, near the foot of the Rich Mountain Road already mentioned.

Polly would later recall that Clyde, who grew up in rural Scott County, was in his natural environment in the mountains. The wood stove for cooking, the oil and gasoline lamps for home lighting were already part of his experience.

Cades Cove ranger Clyde Smith (right in 1949 photo) was fire lookout Russell Whitehead's boss. With Smith was daughter Susie. Harold Edwards (left) was assistant chief Smokies ranger.

The kerosene refrigerator and the butane kitchen stove they later acquired would have been luxuries in his own childhood, he told Polly.

There was a gasoline engine to generate electricity for the ranger's radio that linked him with the fire lookout towers in that section of the park and with park headquarters near Gatlinburg. While the engine was running there was also electricity for a few lights in parts of the house.

Polly said she began to think of herself as a pioneer wife, without the hard work and drudgery of most pioneer wives, and she enjoyed the role.

Clyde taught her to use hand and shoulder weapons and to be especially proficient with a revolver. Hunting was forbidden in the national park, then as now, but she was allowed to shoot copperheads and rattlesnakes, with discretion.

The Smiths spent 15 winters in Cades Cove, and because of the nature of the road they were snowbound many times. "But every snow was like a picnic. We celebrated," Polly said.

They had neighbors in the longtime Cades Cove families who stayed there on farmland leased from the park. Their children became friends and celebrated birthdays, Christmas, Easter and Halloween together, and rode a bus every school day to the nearest schools in Townsend. Daughter Susie, later Susie Reagan of Gatlinburg, was born in 1946, and before Clyde was transferred to Gatlinburg in 1953, she also was riding the bus.

Clyde learned in October of 1953, three months after the move, that he had cancer. He died less than six months later, in March of 1954.

"The Cades Cove years are my memories," Polly said after her own move to Gatlinburg. We took our children almost everywhere we went in those years. It was love pure and simple. I just wish it could have lasted longer."

July 23, 1986

Forge Creek mother taught
respect for family cow

*One milk cow was all his parents kept at one time because of
a scarcity of hay and grain for winter feeding in that time and
place. The recollection is Russell Whitehead's. The time was
just before and after the beginning of the century. The place
was the rocky, shady valley of Forge Creek, above where
it merges with Mill Creek and Abrams Creek in the flatter
lower end of Cades Cove.*

Russell was the sixth or middle child of 11 born to Taylor and
Mary Jane Whitehead. The cow's milk, given twice a day at the gentle
coaxing of Mary Jane's hands, was a main source of family nourish-
ment. Another was cornbread baked
from meal ground at the nearby Cable
Mill.

If whole-grain bread is healthful,
that Cable Mill meal was all of the
grain, and may help account for the fact
that Russell has already lived more than
98 years.

He says the local tradition of grinding only white corn for meal for cornbread goes back at least to his
childhood, and he suspects it may go
back to the time of earliest settlement.

RUSSELL WHITEHEAD
**He grew up in a white
cornbread neighborhood.**

His family's preference was to raise
hickory king corn for meal. He says that even the cut of the millstones has an effect on the quality of meal produced, and that the
Cable millstones made good cornmeal.

"But we did sift the corn bran out of the meal before making
bread. We kept a sifter at the house, and we saved the corn bran for

101

the milk cow," Russell says.

"My mother was the most particular woman about a milk cow that I've ever seen," he says. "If she was able to get to the barn at all, she wouldn't allow anybody else to milk."

To Mary Jane Whitehead, caring about the cow's comfort, cleanliness and general welfare was the same as caring whether her children would eat well each day.

Having a calf at frequent intervals (the gestation period is nine months, as with humans) is what keeps a cow from going dry, and when the family's one cow did go dry, that was sometimes a hardship.

"But most of the time the neighbors divided. And if their cows went dry, we'd divide with them when we had milk," Russell says.

In the time of Russell's childhood, most mountain milk cows had horns. A cow born without horns was called a muley, and, when it was sold, didn't bring as good a price as a milk cow with horns. Russell has never understood why this was so, except it was part of the folklore that a muley cow wouldn't give as much milk.

The Whiteheads, in their succession of family cows, had one that was a natural muley. She also contradicted tradition in that she was a generous giver of milk.

There was a forge hammer, a great chunk of iron that weighed about 400 pounds or more, lying beside Cooper Road where Spence Hill lived, between Cades Cove and Happy Valley. The Whitehead children were awed by that hammer, and would stop to look at it each time they passed, and wonder about the history of it.

One of Russell's brothers suggested one day that their hornless cow looked a lot like that old forge hammer, and from that time on the Whitehead children called her "Old Hammerhead."

They didn't call her that when their mother was in hearing range, for Mary Jane wouldn't allow even spoken disrespect.

"She wouldn't have it," Russell says. "No sir, she wouldn't have it!"

CADES COVE MEN FOUGHT IN WARS 5

She was Granddaddy Rowan's old gun

Russell Whitehead, born in 1888 in Cades Cove, remembers that some of the last owners of muzzle-load rifles used the weapons to hunt wild game and feed their families. Russell, now a Maryville resident, tells us today of two rifles of his acquaintance, both made by members of the Bean family of East Tennessee in their gunsmith shops at or near Jonesboro.

"She was a muzzle loader; she had a flint lock," Russell begins.

"Uncle George Powell always called her *she,* like it was a female. He'd say, 'She was Granddaddy Rowan's old gun, made by Baxter Bean, son of Russell Bean, first white child born on Tennessee soil.'

"He'd tell it all, telling about his old gun.

"She had a little plate of silver about an inch long countersunk in the barrel just behind the rear sight. It said 'B. Bean,' you know, for Baxter Bean. He claimed that little silver plate would give a little light on a dark day – up on the sights. I guess it probably would shine up there a little," Russell says.

George Washington Powell's maternal grandfather was George Washington Rowan, and Powell was named for him. Rowans Creek, on the southeast side of Cades Cove, was named for the family.

Was George Powell a good shot with his rifle?

"I never saw him shoot. I guess he was pretty good, though. All them old-timers used to shoot in matches, you know. I guess he could put a bullet about where he wanted to," Russell says.

"He told me one time that he could see his bullet hole in a board at 100 yards, without glasses. His eyes didn't stay that good, but they stayed good until he got old.

"He took the Knoxville Journal by mail and read just about everything in it. He remembered the most of it. He had the best memory you ever saw. Finally when he got old he had to have glasses to read. But his eyes held up good for a long time."

Russell says that Wilson "Wilse" Burchfield, who was Powell's father-in-law, had another Bean rifle, bigger in bore, and that Wilse called his rifle 'Old Bean.'

Bill Myers and son David with the muzzle-load rifle Bill inherited from his great-grandfather George Powell. Powell had the big apple orchard in Chestnut Flats of Cades Cove.

"He talked to himself all the time. He'd talk to 'Old Bean' and tell it to win him the prize in a shooting match," Russell says.

"I heard Jules Gregg tell about his brother, Leason Gregg, having a store in the old Becky Cable house there in Cades Cove. Leason got in a new hatchet from a Knoxville wholesale house. That was something to be seen back then, a new factory-made hatchet in a country store. Jules said there was a bunch of them there one day, and had their guns, looking at that hatchet and talking about it, and they decided they'd shoot a match for it.

"He said old man Wilse Burchfield went to loading his gun and he said, 'Now, Bean, win me that hatchet.'

"He (Jules Gregg) said Old Bean won her. Uncle Wilse died before my time. I never got to see him. But I've heard my dad (Taylor Whitehead) talk about him a whole lot. My mother (Mary Jane Gregory Whitehead), too. Mother said Wilse Burchfield had the biggest hands and fingers of any man she'd ever seen.

"Old Uncle John Cable from North Carolina was in Cades Cove at his son Fonze Cable's house, and me and Uncle John got to discussing Wilse Burchfield. I told Uncle John what my mother had said about Wilse's hands and fingers.

"Yes," he said. "His hands were so big his fingers looked like hoe handles, and his thumbnails were so big they looked like the old fashioned tucking combs that women used to fasten their hair up with.

"I wish I'd have seen old Uncle Wilse. I'd liked to've seen him and heard him," Russell says.

He says Wilse's rifle, Old Bean, shot a one-ounce, round lead ball. "I believe it was a .56 caliber."

Cove father, sons soldiered together; Powells marched in Union infantry through Civil War

Bill Myers was surprised to find that his Cades Cove great-grandfather, George Washington Powell, was listed awhile as a Union Army deserter in the Civil War. Bill also found that Powell rejoined his outfit and was an unfaltering soldier for the last months of the war.

Sources of Bill's information are microfilmed Army records in the McClung Historical Collection, and notes made by his father, George W. Myers, before his death in 1980.

The Army records show that William Riley Powell, then 44, and his two oldest sons, George W., 22, and William Isaac, 18, enlisted together at Boston, Ky., when the 6th Tennessee Volunteer Infantry Regiment was organized in March and April 1862.

Military maps, also in the McClung Collection, show that Boston, Ky., where hundreds of East Tennesseans volunteered for duty with the Union Army, was directly across the border from Jellico, Tennessee. No town of that name (Boston) in that neighborhood is on today's maps.

The 6th Infantry Regiment would travel 10,000 miles, much of it on foot and some by train or steamboat, before its members were mustered out late in April 1865, a few days after the Civil War ended.

Duties ranged from combat to garrison-keeping and guard duty. The regiment was in the Battle of Atlanta and in Gen. William T. Sherman's March to the Sea. It had roles in the battles of Franklin, Tennessee, and of Nashville.

All three Powells were six feet or taller. A story told about George in the Battle of Nashville is that he picked up a smaller, wounded comrade under one arm and carried him forward without leaving the battlefield.

William Isaac Powell's record shows he was a hospital cook while on garrison duty and a sharpshooter when his company was engaged with the enemy. Bill Myers believes that William Riley Powell taught both sons to shoot with the Baxter Bean flintlock muzzleloader rifle given to him by his father-in-law, George Washington Rowan.

Bill doubts that they carried the rifle with them when they left Cades Cove to walk to Kentucky in March of 1862. They probably

George Washington Myers, born in Cades Cove in 1898, inherited the Bean rifle from his Grandfather Powell.

did some serious thinking as to where would be a safe place to leave it. They needed a place safe from weather, thieves, and Confederate raiders who might (and did) come into Cades Cove while they were away.

The rifle survived and George Powell, as oldest son, inherited it when he returned to Cades Cove after the war. His father, William Riley Powell, would never see Cades Cove again. The father became ill while the regiment was in winter quarters near Knoxville early in 1864. He was in the Army hospital in Knoxville awhile. He may have recovered and returned to duty. He died Aug. 25, 1864, in a hospital at Jeffersonville, Indiana, across the Ohio River from Louisville, Kentucky. Cause of death is listed on his record as dysentery.

William Riley Powell, as a young father in Cades Cove before he left to fight the war, was beginning to be a successful planter and keeper of apple orchards and taught his sons what he had learned.

George returned to the cove and planted 2,000 trees, mostly apple and some peach trees, in the Chestnut Flats section at the west end of Cades Cove. His brother, William Isaac, eventually moved west to the state of Washington and apple orchards were his livelihood there.

Wears Valley Union loyalty
left it target of hostile raiders

Wears Valley in Sevier County at the onset of the Civil War, had 60 households. Out of them came 74 volunteer soldiers for the Union cause, and only one, of record for the Confederate cause.

(The volunteer for the Rebel amy was Bennett King, Jim Shular says. But King had three brothers who fought for the Union.)

The Confederate forces that controlled East Tennessee early in the war, beginning in 1861, resented Wears Valley. They resented all Southern mountain people who wanted to preserve the United States as one nation.

Except for supplying fighting men, Wears Valley did not figure big in the war. Confederate forces raided it several times in hit-and-run cavalry forays.

Some of the raiders were more bandit than soldier. They were thieves intent on stealing horses, food, guns and other valuables. The war was a cover, an excuse for their sack of homes of unprotected families.

James Thomas Lawson was one Wears Valley farmer who favored the Union but did not go away to war. He and his wife, Betsy Mattox Lawson, had eight children, and their needs kept him at home.

The raiders knew about Lawson, whose red hair earned him the nickname "Red Jim" to separate him from another, dark-haired "Black Jim" Lawson. They wanted to capture and maybe kill Red Jim.

They searched his home every time they came to Wears Valley. They burned his corncrib, thinking he might be hid somewhere in it.

Betsy kept a big feather barrel in the loft of their home. Every time a goose, turkey or chicken was plucked, the down and feathers were put in the barrel to be saved for making featherbeds and pillows.

The raiders dumped the barrel once. They knew by the weight of it that there was nobody hiding in it. But they did many unnecessary deeds of vandalism.

There were keen listeners among the Lawson children, and they could hear the sound of horses running from across the valley. Red Jim would head for the Cove Mountain hollow near his home when the raiders came and his sons would help turn the Lawson horses loose in the woods. They went to the woods with the milk cows, too, if they thought they had time.

The house in which Jim and Betsy Lawson and their children survived the war was still standing until a few years ago. It was a log house, deeper from the front to rear than it was wide. Fire destroyed it, and although it hadn't been lived in for many years, there is a sadness in the Lawson family that one of the landmarks of their history is gone.

Betsy Lawson's brother, Valentine Mattox, built the house in which they lived. "V.M. 1829" was found carved in one of the chimney stones.

Valentine Mattox also was a union sympathizer. He was postmaster in Wears Valley before the Civil War.

There's more to the Mattox story. He sheltered Knoxville's firebrand, pro-Union, anti-Confederate newspaper editor, W. G. "Parson" Brownlow, in the fall of 1861. And in sheltering Brownlow, he came close to inciting a Confederate army punitive expedition against Wears Valley.

Cove son wrote goodbye
before he fell in war

Bib overalls were Luke Lawson's natural uniform in the North Carolina logging camps where he had worked several years. But he was careful also about his dress appearance – his suit, shirt, hat and shoes – for church or socializing.

Now, in 1917, he and several Cades Cove neighbors were enlisting in the Army, to go to France and fight the Germans. The Army would take him whether he wore overalls or a dress suit, but Luke decided he would put on the best he had, although the Army would keep it all when they gave him a uniform.

He handed a younger half-sister some money and said, "Here, Pauline, go over to Burchfield's store and get me a pair of sock supporters."

"That was the last little chore I ever did for Luke. That was the last day I ever saw him, and I remember how good he looked," Pauline says. She is now Pauline Lawson Waters and her home for many years has been in East Miller Cove, near Walland.

Luke's last known letter to his family in Cades Cove was written about three weeks before his death. The letter was addressed to his first-cousin, Dulcie Abbott, who is now Dulcie McCaulley of Old Tuckaleechee Pike east of Maryville.

Here is most of the letter:

Sept. 15, 1918

Dear Cousin:

I would be delighted to see and talk with you. I guess I could tell you more than I could write in a week.

I often think of the dear people in the Cove, and if I could travel as fast in my mind, I would make a trip home each day.

111

But as it is! couldn't say yet just when I will be there.

I am so far behind the lines now I can't hear the shells burst. Now believe me, I have been where it was everything but happiness, but I have gotten along all right.

Tell Ella (Tipton) that Mike (her brother) is well. He is working in the kitchen. And all the rest of the boys from the Cove are well.

Tell Ira I am real sorry to hear of his sickness. Tell him to try to get well, and when I get back we will be together and have a good time. And if we never meet again on Earth I want to meet him in a better world than this.

Tell all the people hello for me. Write me soon, and a long letter. Tell me all the good news.

As ever,

Luke Lawson

goodbye

The *Ira* that Luke mentioned was Dulcie's brother, Ira Abbott. He was indeed seriously ill, with tuberculosis of the bone. But he recovered and lived many more years, Dulcie says.

Of the several letters Luke is known to have written in the months he was in Europe, this was the first to say *goodbye* at the end.

He was a corporal in the 117th Infantry Regiment, 30th Division. The regiment was commanded by Col. Cary F. Spence of Knoxville.

On Sept. 29, two weeks after Luke wrote the letter, the 117th was in the battle of Bellicourt where the Allies broke Germany's Hindenburg Line.

Beginning Oct. 5, 1918, the regiment was in the battle for Piedmont and Busigny, and it was in that fighting, three days later on Oct. 8, that Luke was killed.

Another Cades Cove soldier, Alex Gregory, saw him die. Luke was hand-holding a machine gun on his knees in a shell-hole, firing it, when an enemy bullet hit him in the forehead, Alex said when he returned from the war.

Luke was buried in a temporary grave in Europe, as were most soldiers who died in battle. He had made it known before he left home that if he should be killed, he wanted to be brought back to Cades Cove for burial.

So as soon as the war ended, Nov. 11, 1918, a month and three days after Luke was killed, his father, Jasper Lawson, began pushing for return of the body.

Two and a half years later, in April of 1921, the coffin arrived at the Little River Railroad depot that was then called Riverside, at the lower end of Tuckaleechee Cove.

There was a soldier escort with the body, and the coffin was hauled across Rich Mountain in a horse-drawn wagon, over a steep road that was still too primitive for a motor hearse.

Jasper was wondering if the body in the coffin was indeed his son. He asked the soldiers to open the box so he could see for himself, and they said he'd have to have a court order.

So the father went to Justice of the Peace Andrew Witt Shields, Cades Cove member of the Blount County Quarterly Court, and Shields wrote an order that the coffin be opened.

Kara Gregory, now of Maryville and then a young boy in Cades Cove, was there when Jasper viewed the skeleton of his son, the bullet hole in the forehead and the metal identification tags with Luke's name and serial number.

Squire Shields' daughter Norma was a young girl the year of the funeral. She is now Mrs. Glenn Cunningham, of the Prospect community of Blount County, north of Chilhowee Mountain.

"Everybody in Cades Cove must have been there," Norma says. "The Methodist Church was crowded and there were people looking in the windows.

"It was a sad thing – it was a tragedy. I cried and cried, and nobody tried to stop me."

Christmas gave sanctuary to stricken Blount soldier

Remember, please even if you were born after it, that there was a war, in the second quarter of the 20th Century in which many soldiers were dying, or nearly dying, which is often the same. To be close to death in war is sometimes reversible, although not always happily so. In the case of one Blount County soldier, the outcome is one that fits Christmas.

Perry Shields was born in 1925 in a small rented house in Mitchell Hollow at Townsend. His mother was Alice Dorsey from Dry Valley. His father was Fred D. Shields, a worker at the big sawmill of Little River Lumber Co.

Fred was from a Cades Cove family with a strong work ethic. His father, Dave Shields, owned 550 cove acres on Wildcat Branch, all of it surrounded by a fence seven rails high. Dave and his children split the rails from chestnut logs.

Some of the Shieldses were combative and aggressive. But they also had reputations as workers. Perry was introspective.

He was a medical aide with the 104th (Timberwolf) Infantry Division when mortar shrapnel shattered his left leg, on Nov. 29, 1944. The fighting was on the German Autobahn between Eschweiler and Cologne.

Five days later gangrene had developed and the leg was amputated in a field hospital, in the high school building at Aachen.

The Battle of the Bulge was developing, and German buzz bombs began to hit around the hospital. The orderlies hung blankets over the windows to shield against flying glass, and moved the patients to litters under their beds. But soon the building had to be evacuated.

Perry was put in an ambulance, beside an unconscious flash-burn victim, to be moved from the front.

The enemy were focusing their fire on road intersections. There was only the driver and his two patients, neither able to move from his litter. The driver left the ambulance and took cover at each shelling, and returned when it subsided.

"Where are we? What's happening?" Perry would ask. The driver rotated his answers:

"Hellfire, soldier, how would I know?

"Good God, soldier, how would I know?"

They reached the hospital train on a siding at Liege, Belgium, at midnight. A dazzling light shone through the ambulance windows. The train, painted white, was lighted by big searchlights, so the enemy would know it was a hospital train and not bomb it.

When Perry awoke next morning, he was being moved to a hospital in one of the grand, lush hotels of Paris. Days later he was back in an ambulance, to be moved to Le Bourget airport, where Charles A. Lindbergh had landed 17 years earlier, after his pioneer flight from America.

Perry and nearly 200 others, all unable to leave their litters without being carried, were to be moved in transport planes to a hospital near Liverpool, England. It would be Perry's first airplane ride, but it would be another four days and three nights before the weather over England would allow the flight.

Paris, meanwhile, was beautiful in the sunshine. On the ride to the airport from the hotel hospital he saw the Eiffel Tower through the back window of the ambulance.

In a hangar at the airport, his litter was put beside the burn victim with whom he rode from Aachen. There was a stench that caused him to worry that what was left of his leg had become gangrenous again.

Two Army nurses and two soldier orderlies worked all the hours they could stay awake to tend their patients, apportion their medicine, feed them, dress their wounds.

Perry and 17 other soldiers, one planeload, arrived at Liverpool on Christmas Eve. They were taken to a hospital in the nearby town of Satan. A nurse named Keppler divided her Christmas whiskey ration with them, one big shot for each soldier.

It was Perry's first drink of whiskey. He had drunk a few beers along. He was 19 years old. According to a letter he wrote to a friend, the first drink made him "skunk drunk, flat on my back. I was down to 109 pounds. I was all ears and eyeballs."

Perry Shields today, with an artificial left leg, weighs 185 pounds. He has recovered remarkably from the physical and psychological wounds of war. In the beginning the recovery was slow and uncertain.

He graduated from Duke University after the war, and then from its law school in 1950. He and Bonnie were married in 1951. She is a proprietor of the Pioneer House Restaurant near McGhee Tyson Airport.

Their children are Bailey, a Townsend businessman; daughter Leslie, a graduate of Emory University and the UT law school, now a lawyer with the Kramer firm of Knoxville; daughter Beth, Vanderbilt graduate in mechanical engineering, now employed with the Army Corps of Engineers at Louisville, Ky.

Perry began his career as an agent with the Internal Revenue Service. Then he became a lawyer in the office of its chief counsel. He left the IRS in 1956 to practice tax law, and was in private practice in Knoxville until February of 1982.

He was then appointed by the president to be a federal judge of the U.S. Tax Court, "with the advice and consent of the U.S. Senate."

Thank you, Perry, after we have known one another 38 years, for letting me tell some of your story. I told you I wouldn't be maudlin, and I kept my promise. This is for the thousands of others who didn't intend to be heroes, but tried to do what was expected of them, in whatever war they found themselves.

– Vic Weals

November 8, 1984

Innovations Made
Mountain Life Easier

6

Car customized for a bear hunter

Chevrolet switched from four-cylinder to six-cylinder engines for all of its cars beginning with the 1929 models. By then it was making mostly closed cars with windows that could be cranked up and down: four-door sedans, two-door "coaches" and coupes with no rear seat.

There were customers out there who thought closed cars were

Magazine advertising illustration is of Chevrolet's 1929 four-door open touring car. The company made only 1,800 of them, and Cades Cove native John McCaulley bought one to drive to work in North Carolina.

more dangerous in a wreck than open cars were, reasoning that a closed car would be more difficult to get out of.

There was an East Tennessee incident in the 1920s in which a new closed car rolled off a ferry into Little Tennessee River.

All the occupants were drowned, trapped inside, and the newspaper story questioned the general safety of riding in closed cars.

The Model T Ford had been the predominant vehicle of the 20 years leading up to 1929, and most of the Ts were of open touring or runabout body styles. The big trend, though, late in the 1920s, was suddenly to closed cars. They offered greater comfort through more seasons. Their windows could be quickly raised against dust or sudden rain. Their doors could be locked against intruders.

Most people who bought a new car in 1929 bought a closed body model. Chevrolet manufactured only 1,800 four-door open tourings in that model year. It was a final, token gesture to motorists who craved fresh air more than comfort and who often leaned out the side to see where they were headed.

John T. McCaulley, Cades Cove farmer and Smoky Mountain guide to campers and hunters, bought a new, four-door open touring. It had no heater but came with a set of canvas and isinglass side curtains that could be snapped into place in five to 10 minutes.

The owner of such a car could keep the side curtains in place all the time and not see well through the murky isinglass. Or he could keep the curtains folded under the rear seat and stand in the open to put them on after rain began to fall.

One of the McCaulley daughters, Mayme McCaulley Tipton, says it was the first car her father owned. He was 48 years old.

One of the McCaulley sons, John Earl McCaulley, remembers his father counting out $520 from a roll of cash in his pocket to pay for the car in full. The bills were $20 gold certificates, 26 of them.

John Sr. had been working at one of the Aluminum Company of America's hydroelectric projects. This one was in North Carolina, across the main ridge of the Smokies from his Cades Cove home on a branch of Forge Creek.

John was living in a company work camp and had been walking home weekends across the mountain near Gregory Bald by the shortest route. Now that he owned a car he would be driving home, weekends only, by a much longer route.

His new road home followed what is now U.S. 129, an end run of the Smokies from Tapoco to Maryville. The rest of the route was one he had traveled often with wagon and mule team. It was the historic

Tuckaleechee Pike to Townsend and Dry Valley, and the old road across Rich Mountain. For years it was the only usable road in and out of Cades Cove.

The man who had leaned on the wind of the high Smokies most of his life enjoyed his new car. He gave it one custom touch that may have been unique among all Chevrolets. He upholstered the inside door panels with the hide of a bear.

When John and Rutha McCaulley bought a new vehicle, in 1936, they chose a Chevrolet pickup with a closed cab and a factory-installed heater. They sold the old open touring car to the family of Rufus Coada, neighbors who stayed in Cades Cove many years after the McCaulleys left.

The Coadas shortened the cloth top, sawed off the rear end of the body and built a small pickup bed in its place. They later sold the car to still another family.

The last time anybody remembers seeing it, the front doors were still upholstered in bearskin.

Howard Sparks remembers Cable Mill

*Howard Sparks remembered when the Cable Mill in Cades Cove
included a waterpower sawmill beside the grist mill. It was a
sash saw, a straight blade kept moving up and down
by an eccentric wheel.*

Beautiful cherry lumber in great widths was sawed at the Cable
Mill and shipped to the coffin factory at Maryville. That went on as
recently as early in the 20th Century.

The mill was water-powered. An eccentric wheel kept the straight
blade moving up and down until it had sawed amost to the end of
the log.

When all the boards were sawed almost to the end, the end was
sawed off, allowing the boards to fall free.

Sparks said that Becky Cable's brother Jim was generally thought
of as being the operator of both the grain mill and the sawmill. But it
was Jim's wife, Susannah Burchfield Cable, who often ran both mills
unassisted, he said.

She could turn the ratchet to move a heavy, big-diameter log into
starting place on the carriage. She could heft the sacks of corn and
meal to and from the backs of horses of the mill's patrons.

When there was plenty of water in the race, both the grist mill and
the sawmill could be operated at the same time. There once was built,
by hand labor through tough mountain rock, a canal from Gorge Creek
to Mill Creek. The purpose was to add to the flow of water to the
Cable Mill.

Howard Sparks was born in Cades Cove in 1892. His aunt Alice
White married one of the Cables, and Howard as a boy visited the mill
often, and stayed many a night in what is now labeled the Becky Cable
house in the Great Smoky Mountains National Park visitor complex
at the lower end of the cove.

The house was moved to its present, more convenient location in the 1950s. It long stood beside Mill Creek on the Forge Creek Road.

The Cable Mill is said to have been started entirely as a grist mill, grinding corn into meal, about the time of the Civil War. The owner, John P. Cable, later added a wheat mill, and had bolting cloths to remove the bran and shorts, thus to produce a white flour of sorts.

Sparks said it was his understanding that the flour milling did not prove profitable. Cornbread was the bread of that time and place, and there was not yet much demand for "lightbread." Storekeepers stocked enough white flour to meet local demand.

The long, steep, twisting road in and out of Cades Cove, over

Cable Mill was built by John P. Cable about 1865. It was started as a grist mill, grinding corn into meal. Its waterwheel later powered a sash saw to cut logs into lumber. The National Park Service restored the grist mill in 1936, with the help of broadax artisans Tom and Jerry Hearon of Happy Valley in Blount County. Since restoration it has ground corn into meal for sale to Cades Cove visitors in the warm months.

Rich Mountain through Rich Mountain Gap, also limited the Cable sawmill to producing lumber that brought a high price. Cherry skidded down from the higher hollows of the Smokies was one of these. Cherry was prized for making furniture, coffins and fireplace mantles. Tipton Sugar Cove in a side hollow of Forge Creek yielded a fabulous stand of black cherry timber, all of it sawed slowly by waterpower at the Cable mill. That lumber, too, was hauled to Maryville in wagons.

Sparks said two or three portable steam sawmills were moved into the cove after Little River Railroad came to Townsend about 1902. The wagon haul was shortened now, with most lumber out of the cove delivered to the train depot at Riverside, at the lower end of Tuckaleechee Cove.

Still, only the higher-priced woods were being sawed. "Yellow pine didn't bring enough for us to make anything on it. White pine sold higher, and stands of white pine were cut all around Cades Cove," Sparks said.

When he was 12 years old, in 1904, Howard was driving a team, helping his father George Sparks haul wagonloads of lumber from Cades Cove across Rich Mountain to Riverside.

No logging railroad ever reached Cades Cove, but there probably would have been one if it had not been for the creation of Great Smoky Mountains National Park beginning in the 1920s. The Morton Butler family of Chicago had bought tracts totaling nearly 25,000 acres, mostly uncut timberland south of Abrams Creek beginning at the lower end of Cades Cove. The Babcock interests, who were already logging 100,000 acres south of Little Tennessee River, were looking at the Butler tract when the national park movement became serious in the 1920s. If the Babcocks had bought it, they would have built a railroad up Abrams Creek from a connection with Southern Railway at Chilhowee.

Little River Lumber Company's rails from Townsend up West Prong of Little River and Laurel Creek reached almost to Crib Gap, through which Cades Cove visitors now pass on the road completed since World War II. While the railroad stayed there, there was some hauling of lumber out of the cove in that direction, to be loaded on trains there, Sparks said.

But even without a railroad into the cove proper, many of its more accessible hollows were logged by local families. The logs were sawed into lumber at the Cable waterpower mill and at the steam portable sawmills brought in later.

Picture from the album of Dulcie Abbott McCaulley is of her father John Abbott's steam-powered sawmill in Cades Cove early in the century. Unidentified man second from left was firing the boiler and held a length of slab for fuel. Dulcie said most of the lumber her father sawed was hauled out of the Cove in horse-drawn wagons across Cades Cove Mountain and Rich Mountain.

Almost all of it that reached the outside world was hauled tediously across Rich Mountain in horse-drawn wagons. In the last days of private land ownership in Cades Cove, some lumber was hauled by motor truck. "That was awful hard on the trucks we had back then," Sparks said.

A grist mill with self-control

Tommy Boring ran a grist mill on Abrams Creek near Happy Valley at a place called the "Rich Woods," below Cades Cove and in what is now Great Smoky Mountains National Park.

Tommy liked to fish, and even when he wasn't fishing he didn't have the patience to stand and watch the water slowly turn the wheel, and the wheel turn one stone against the other, slowly to grind the corn into meal at the rate of two or three bushels per hour.

I. M. Hawkins, who grew up around the Cable Mill in Cades Cove, says the Cable Mill in those days would grind about three bushels an hour when water to turn the mill was plentiful, and would slow down to about two bushels per hour when the water was low.

But if Tommy didn't stand there and watch, and if all the corn in the hopper ran out and there was nothing to separate the stones, the turning stone would start turning so fast that both stones would soon be ground to pieces.

So he rigged a governor from a pair of poles. As long as the mill turned slowly – and that's the way it would turn with corn to grind – it was allowed to keep turning. But when the mill speeded up, indicating that the corn in the hopper was all ground, the homemade governor would trip and lower the mill gate to shut off water to the undershot wheel. Thus, with no water to turn the wheel, the mill would halt and the stones wouldn't grind themselves to pieces, and Tommy Boring could go on fishing without worry.

Or, he could start the mill before he went to bed at night and fall asleep secure in knowing that the mill would turn itself off automatically when the corn was ground.

Millers and millwrights from miles around came to see Tommy Boring's automatic grist mill in action. He didn't intend to patent it and they were free to study it and copy it – to build one exactly like it.

But they'd better not ask Tommy to draw them any plans. That's why he had invented the automatic mill – to be able to get away from it. Tommy Boring last operated his mill in 1927. Ten years later, on New Year's Day of 1937, he was living with his grandson Lonnie at Six Mile, across Chilhowee Mountain from Happy Valley.

After a meal of hog jowl and peas on that New Year's Day, Tommy, then 86, announced to the family that he needed only one more thing to make the day special. He said he would walk across Chilhowee Mountain, seven miles, to see his beloved mill again. He made it there September 24, 1959.

Jerry Hearon's telegraph water system

I had come to Happy Valley to see Jerry Hearon. This Happy Valley is between Chilhowee Mountain and the western tip of Great Smoky Mountains National Park. We get there by taking U.S. Highway 129 South past the end of Chilhowee Mountain and turning north on Happy Valley Road.

I hoped Jerry would have time to tell us about his water system.

Jerry Hearon dips a drink from the original galvanized bucket of his homemade water system.

It's the talk of that Blount County neighborhood which many consider to be an extension of Cades Cove. Abrams Creek begins in Cades Cove and flows generally west past Happy Valley and into Little Tennessee River.

Jerry was at home. He had started down the path to the mailbox as I drove up. "Probably don't have any mail anyhow," he said. He walked back to the house with me without finishing his errand.

Until about 1920 Jerry had to walk down a steep hill to the spring. Then he began to figure and he put up a heavy wire all the way from his back yard to the spring.

Now he rigged a pair of wheels to run on the wire. And he hung a bucket from the set of wheels. The bucket would slide down 100 yards of wire until it hit the water in the spring. When the bucket touched water, it started to tip over. Once tipped, the bucket fills and Jerry gets the full bucket back up the hill by cranking the windlass.

That's all there is to it and it beats climbing up and down that steep bank every time Jerry wants a cold drink of water. One of his visitors called it a telegraph water system because it delivers water by wire.

The brothers Tom and Jerry Hearon worked as a team of broadax artisans along the 70-mile length of the new national park. They hewed logs to build the cabins that were living quarters at fire lookout towers. They built wooden bridges and other rustic structures in the park. They rebuilt the Cable Mill, including its precisely weighted and balanced wheel. They walked to their work, sometimes up mile-high mountains from the eastern end of the park above Big Pigeon River to the western end near their Happy Valley home.

Both men were great walkers. They hoofed it into Knoxville, not less than 40 miles by the shortest route, to buy their first Winchester rifles years ago. They often shanked it over Chilhowee Mountain into Maryville. Jerry remembers walking to Maryville in three hours and 20 minutes when he was a young boy – says he "had a bad toothache and was in a hurry to get to the dentist."

We take a giant step from 1951 to the year 2001 and return to Happy Valley to find that Verl Hearon and wife Sue now have the home where Jerry lived and that they, with the help of son Jerry, have restored the original water system to working condition. Caleb, 10-year-old grandson of Verl and Sue, had also become interested and won a Blount County Schools award for his illustrated history of what he calls "Uncle Jerry's Waterwheel." Pencil sketches were done by Earl Hill, retired from the Blount County Highway Engineering Department. Earl is a great-nephew of the original Jerry and as a young boy cranked up water with the windlass, to drink and to amuse himself.

Verl and Sue rebuilt the home sometime ago with a new well as their everyday water supply. But in the first years of their marriage they drew water, even for washing clothes, up the wire from the spring deep in the hollow 100 yards away, the length of a football field.

A creek ran through their photo lab

Andrew Shields, in Cades Cove early in the 20th Century, owned a little amateur photographer's outfit for printing and developing pictures. Luther Abbott took a liking to it; Andrew sold it to him for $3.

Dulcie Abbott McCaulley

There were trays for the developer and fixer solution. There was a printing frame to hold the negative in contact with the photographic paper. There may have been an oil-burning red safelight. The Abbotts had no electricity and except for a very few families who owned a Delco home-generating system, there was no electricity in Cades Cove.

The photographic paper was exposed by holding the glass printing frame to the light of a window for a certain length of time, or even by taking it outdoors. After the exposed print was developed and fixed in the chemicals, it was taken to the creek and washed in repeated changes of water. Luther was one of seven sons and there were three daughters, the children of John and Rhoda Lawson Abbott. The boys ruled the darkroom and their sisters were forbidden to go about it.

"But I'd catch them gone and slip in and develop my own pictures," says Dulcie Abbott McCaulley. She and her brother Ernest Abbott (in 1977) are the only survivors among the 10 children. A trick Dulcie liked to play on them was to take a negative of one of the boys and another negative of one of the Cades Cove girls their age and print them side-by-side on the same piece of photo paper. Then she'd leave the finished, dried print where the right people would be certain to find it.

The Abbott boys seldom developed their own negatives. They sent the exposed film to Thompson's in Knoxville by mail and in a very few days they'd get it back with one set of prints the same size as the negatives. Always black and white in that day, of course. If they wanted extra copies of a certain picture, they'd print their own in the home darkroom.

Dulcie remembers cutting a design from paper with scissors and laying the paper on the negative in the printing frame as she exposed the photo paper. She has the picture in her album still. The fact that the print is in good condition, hasn't yellowed or faded, shows that she did everything about right as to developing, fixing and washing the print.

Dulcie married Millard McCaulley, the oldest son of John and Rutha Myers McCaulley. Dulcie and Millard had been married more than 50 years when he died in 1976. Three of their four children were born in Cades Cove before they moved out in the '30s to make way for the Great Smoky Mountains National Park.

One of Dulcie's nostalgic pleasures these days, at her home on Tuckaleechee Pike out of Maryville, is to share memories with her children and grandchildren via pictures.

Cabbage an ideal Cove crop

Howard Sparks was 90 years old in 1982 and had lived only his first 14 years, less than one-sixth of his life, in Cades Cove. Yet it was the Smoky Mountain years that younger people wanted to know about when they came to visit.

"Of course I went back to the cove, down through the years. I hunted bear on Thunderhead with my Uncle Tom Sparks, and with Fonz Cable.

"I visited my Uncle Dave Sparks a lot, and his wife Mary. I always felt welcome there. Dave stayed on in Cades Cove after the national park came. He died in the cove," Howard said.

He connected most of the big adventures of his childhood to trips to the main ridge of the Smokies above the cove, and to wagon journeys to Maryville and Knoxville, both of which were awesomely big places from his view.

His father, George Sparks, was an enterpriser who was seldom without some unusual project for making a living. George and his wife, Rachel White, had nine children, Howard the oldest.

Even after the railroad came early in the century to Townsend, across the mountain from Cades Cove, George continued to haul produce of farm and forest by horse-drawn wagon all the way to Knoxville to sell on Market Square. As soon as he was old enough to endure the hard living of a long wagon journey, Howard became his father's traveling companion. "I was about 10 years old when I made the first one," he said.

They traveled the steep road across Cades Cove Mountain and Rich Mountain into the Little River Valley at the lower end of Tuckaleechee Cove. They followed a wagon road down Little River to the neighborhood of Wildwood and Nails Creek. They camped at Goddard Hill there at the end of the first long day.

Remainder of the distance by historic Martin Mill Pike to Knoxville was shorter than what they had already traveled. They would be in Knoxville in time to park the wagon on Market Square and lodge the horses in one of the nearby livery stables. Sometimes there'd be enough of the afternoon left to do some selling.

If they sold enough from the wagon there'd be room to sleep in it that night. If there wasn't room they'd sleep in the livery stable or even in the livery stable office. Cost of a hotel room would have taken too much of the profit of the trip. Howard couldn't recall that his father ever considered registering at a hotel.

One of the big excitements of the visit, for a boy, was to be able to eat at a restaurant. Cost of a plate lunch was 15 cents.

None of the female members of the family made any of the wagon trips to sell produce. Early in the summer the wagon might be loaded with cabbage, one of the more prolific vegetable crops of Cades Cove. Cabbage would last without refrigeration, rain didn't hurt it and it was easily transportable.

Cabbage chopped into a slaw with only vinegar and salt to season it was a favorite raw or salad vegetable of the day. New-crop cabbage was a ready seller on Market Square, Howard said.

Most of the autumn wagon trips were to haul apples and chestnuts to market. Sound apples brought 50 cents a bushel and chestnuts sold for $4 a bushel. The apples were from planted orchards on the slopes just above the cove. The chestnuts were from great stands of natural forest just under the mile-high crest of the Smokies.

Howard didn't know why his father sold the family's Cades Cove farm of 120 acres. But he did sell it, in October of 1906, to Pete Myers for $2,000. That was long before there was any serious move to create a national park in the Smokies.

Howard said his family were not pioneers in the fact that they moved *out* of Cades Cove. Dozens of families moved out in the almost 100 years of white settlement before the Sparkses left.

SMOKIES ALWAYS ATTRACTED CAMPERS

7

Campers thronged top of Old Smoky

Ernest Tipton, after a working life in construction of big and small industrial buildings from Idaho to Ohio, is back in his native Smokies. He lives on Old Cades Cove Road out of Townsend, within view of the same Rich Mountain he crossed many times as a boy and young man, to reach the main ridge of the Smokies beyond.

Ernest's sister, Belle Tipton Emert, lives on a hilltop in West Miller Cove. Her home allows a direct view of the Rocky Top end of Thunderhead Mountain, lofty summering place of her early married years with Ira Emert who died young in 1938.

Belle and Ira owned a general store at Walland in the years the tannery was operated there. She also managed the Walland post office as postmaster 25 years until retirement.

The light, one-horse wagon that was the store's delivery vehicle was also their camping conveyance. It was fitted with a tongue so a team of mules could be hitched to it. The mules were more sure-footed than a horse would have been for the climb up the steep, rocky Bote Mountain trail to Spence Field, which joins Thunderhead Mountain on the west.

"We almost always invited friends and family on our camping trips. There'd be as many as 50 people on some of them," Belle says. The wagon carried skillets, buckets, dutch ovens and other tools for cooking and eating. It carried fresh ears of corn, new potatoes and green beans from the garden, and at this time of year at least one sack of early apples.

"We lived out of the garden back then. And that was most of what we took camping," Ernest says. "We went up there two or three times a year, and planned to stay about a week each time. Sometimes there'd be enough grub left that we could stay longer.

"We cooked over an open fire with a sheet of metal over it for a cooking surface. We'd have fried apples for breakfast, along with the usual eggs, bacon and biscuits. Fried apples make a memorable breakfast. We took a few things from the grocery store, too. We'd have hoop cheese and crackers, coffee and condensed milk.

"I didn't drink coffee in those years, but I remember they made it by pouring the coffee into the water and boiling it. The grounds went to the bottom, and the coffee was poured from the top of the pot. But anybody who drank it also swallowed some of the grounds."

Belle's and Ernest's brother Mynatt and sister Gladys (now Gladys Hatcher) were regulars on many of the trips. Their sister Tressie went a time or two, and their mother Elizabeth made it once. Their father John Tipton, a Townsend farmer, was their most frequent and eager companion.

Belle's and Ira's oldest sons, Paul and Fred, seldom missed a trip after they reached their sixth birthdays. The youngest, John, was 5 years old when he camped the first time, in 1940, two years after the death of his father.

Most of the campers who could control a saddle horse rode one to the top. Those who went by horse rode across Rich Mountain into Cades Cove, and then rode the trail to Spence Field from the upper end of the Cove, starting place where the picnic ground now is. Those who drove the mule team walked beside the wagon more than they rode in it. Sometimes they helped the mules by lifting the wagon over boulders.

And they rode a different route, through Dry Valley past the Dunn place, through Schoolhouse Gap and the White Oak Sink, across Laurel Creek and up the Bote Mountain Trail to the camping place on the North Carolina side of Spence Field, near the spring and near where the hikers' shelter now stands beside the Appalachian Trail.

"That was worth the trip up there – to be able to drink that good water for a week," Belle says.

Compiled

Prof. Duncan 'at home in the Cove'

Five hiking clubs met in Cades Cove of the Great Smoky Mountains for a "convention" of hiking clubs. Smoky Mountain Hiking Club was host and the others were the Potomac hiking organization from Washington, D. C., and the Atlanta, Asheville, and Kingsport hiking clubs.

The feature of this year's meet was a tour of the Cove with Henry Rankin Duncan, professor of animal husbandry at University of Tennessee, as guide. "Prof" Duncan, regarded as an authority on the lay of local mountains, the Smokies and the Chilhowees which flank the Smokies to the north and west, had been tagged the "Sage of the Chilhowees." He's very much at home in the Cove, though. And he's known many of its inhabitants down through the years.

The hiking clubs do more than just walk through the woods, Professor Duncan said. They are also interested in the preservation of the lore of the places they visit.

Smoky Mountain Hiking Club, in 1930, had come to Cades Cove the night before and stayed in a lodge built by the John W. Oliver family. Picture early the next morning was by A.G. Roth.

It's 1951 and we're on Gregory Bald

We rested at the end of a hike to Gregory Bald in the Great Smoky Mountains. We awoke when four boys from Cades Cove arrived at the shelter along about dusk. They were Billy, Kermit, and Bob Coada, and Darrell Cable, all on horseback. They had sleeping bags and spread them in the open near the shelter on the legendary Gregory Bald grass. Their mounts were tethered where they could nibble at the same delicacy nearby.

Breaking camp, Bill Kegley douses the fire as the hikers prepare to set out for home. Jimmy Long (left) assembles his pack while Lester Clark waits with another can of water to throw on the ashes. Boys in background live in Cades Cove and came up the mountain late the evening before on horseback. Left to right are Billy Coada, Darrell Cable and Bob Coada. They also camped here for the night.

All these boys are woodsmen, having been brought up in the heart of the Smokies. Their families farm Cove land leased from the Park Service.

I supposed that horses would be the ideal transportation for a person traveling these mountain trails. Not so, said the boys. For unless you're a veteran horseperson, the ride may leave you with more sore joints than if you had walked.

Horses in the mist — **Darrell Cable and the Coada brothers, Bill, Kermit and Bob are cooled by a cloud on Gregory Bald in August 1951. At the time they lived in Cades Cove. All four are alive and well 50 years later, in 2001.**

Another factor is that some of these trails are quite steep and rocky-rough in places. A horse could be injured easily with the reins in inexpert hands. Hugh Hoss, Journal staffer who spent considerable time hiking the Smokies, advocates the burro as an ideal animal for these trails. He alleges that the burro is more sure-footed and less liable to injure itself, that it can carry heavy loads, and that it can subsist on the grass it will nibble along the trails.

Those are but some of the things we think about while rubbing horse liniment on a charley-horse. So back to sleep, but not for long. The others are out early this morning. Bill Kegley stayed up all night, watching the fire and enjoying it.

We broke camp about 6:30 a.m. and started up the trail to the highest part of the bald. We were traveling a different route home. After Gregory we descended to the grass-carpeted oak forest of Sheep Pen Gap. The sheep pen itself that had been photographed 21 years earlier by Dutch Roth was no longer distinguishable. Then we climbed again, this time to Parson Bald.

The clouds had passed and the early morning sun was beaming at us from the direction of North Carolina. Some of our group lagged behind to feast on it. The valleys were still filled with fog, looking somewhat like lakes with mountaintops as islands.

Toll gate house on Old Tennessee River Turnpike (Maryville to Franklin) near Deals Gap in Blount County about 1906. George Davis and daughters, Mary and Dixie.

The men who invited us on this hike are natives of the Blount County shadow of Chilhowee Mountain. Bill Kegley is a sawmill man. Jimmy Long, Joe Roddy, Chester Willocks, Robert, Lonas, Luther, and Lester Clark work at ALCOA. The younger hikers who will be reporting back to school next week were Clyde Clark, Clell Willocks, and Jim Swaney. All spent the evening on the bald and most of the rest of the night talking about the wonder of the place. This morning, on the way home, they refuse to be in a hurry.

After Parson Bald our journey is mostly downhill. We're still following the blue-paint blazes on rocks and trees that mark the Appalachian Trail. But presently we come to Dalton Gap, and Lonas Clark says he knows a trail that leads to the Toll Gate. It will be easier traveling than the ridgeline path to Deals Gap, he says.

The kudzu vines have nearly blocked Lonas' short-cut, but once we break through the first few yards the going gets easier. Finally we reach the Toll Gate, three hours and seven minutes after we left the camp below Gregory Bald. Total walking distance, for two days, was about 12 miles.

Raymond Thompson from Christie Hill isn't due to drive here and pick us up until noon. So we spend the rest of the morning eating and sleeping and vowing to take another hike before long.

Rocky Top! Home sweet home to sheep, mules, cattle and hogs

There is a Rocky Top, Tennessee, and right next to it there's a Rocky Top, North Carolina.

Carl "G. I." Davis says Rocky Top is the highest pinnacle of Thunderhead Mountain on the main divide of the Smokies and that the Tennessee-North Carolina line runs "almost through the middle of Rocky Top."

Carl is a Great Smoky Mountains National Park ranger recently retired. In his Cades Cove years he made possibly 200 tripes to Thunderhead, sometimes on foot but usually by Jeep up the Bote Mountain trail. The vehicle path ended at Spence Field, and he climbed on foot the short remaining distance to Rocky Top.

The trail, entered through a locked gate from the Laurel Creek road into Cades Cove, was open to National Park Service vehicles through most of Carl's tenure. Now it is closed even to those vehicles.

Brothers James (left) and Carson Francis were as curious about the unfettered mules they found roaming Rocky Top as the mules were about them. These young mules had been left on the free range to grow and fatten, at little expense to their unknown owners. All of these pictures from Herbert Webster, one of the Rocky Top hikers in October 1928.

"Nobody ever lived on Rocky Top that I've heard of," Carl says. "The wind and the lightning, and just getting there, made it a forbidding place to live.

"People did range their livestock up there in summer and up until early fall. They turned their cattle and sheep, and even their mules and hogs, on all that high range. But that was 50 years ago or more," Carl says.

Herbert M. Webster walked to Thunderhead and Rocky Top 53 years ago, in October of 1928, in search of the native American chest-

The late James A. Francis made this picture of sheep beginning to stir on a cold October 1928 dawn on mile-high Thunderhead Mountain, just under Rocky Top. Francis and companions had camped the night before at the edge of Spence Field below this point. Those who remember the era of livestock grazing on the bald range of the Smokies say that sheep kept to higher ground, while cattle browsed in the grassy forests at the shoulder of the mountain.

nut that then grew abundantly on the ridges under the main divide.

The blight has killed all the chestnut trees in the years since, and even their great white trunk skeletons that stood through years of mountain storm are mostly gone today.

"They were living giants in 1928," Herbert says, "several feet in circumference and with branches so lofty it hurt to look up at them."

Herbert and all of his mountain-climbing companions that weekend, Bill Wolfe, Carson Francis, Jim Francis, Max Dance and Leonard Davidson, were employees of House-Hasson, a Knoxville-based wholesale hardware company.

They drove from Knoxville in Wolfe's Star automobile. From

the lower end of Tuckaleechee Cove, near Kinzel Springs, they followed the steep, twisting road across Rich Mountain that was then the only automobile road into Cades Cove.

Creation of a national park in the Smokies was under way in

Hikers to Thunderhead in October of 1928 found a crude but stout pole pyramid on its highest pinnacle, Rocky Top. They never did learn the purpose of the pyramid, but believe it may have been a place to scout for fires.
Belle Tipton Emert who hiked the mountains with her family about the same time, believes the pole pyramid was a survey marker of the Tennessee-North Carolina line.

1928, but the land buyers hadn't reached Cades Cove in force, except on exploratory trips. The Cove was still well populated and Jim Wolfe knew a number of its residents. He stopped frequently to say hello to those who lived by the roadside.

"At some of the stops we were challenged by any number of hounds, as we would have been while traveling almost anywhere in the country at that time," Herbert says.

"The owner would yell at his dogs and they'd slink under the porch to continue barking.

"We parked the car in the yard of one of Bill's friends. This was on the east end of Cades Cove where the picnic ground is now. We headed for the Bote Mountain trail by which people drove their livestock to and from the bald pastures – on Rocky Top, Spence Field and Russell Field."

Owners of land through which hikers passed warned them to "put up the bars."

"That meant to replace the split chestnut rails which we let down to go through the pasture fences."

They had left Knoxville at 1 p.m., after their employer's Saturday closing. After the drive to the Cove and the eight-mile walk up Bote Mountain, it was dark when they reached Spence Field just under the crest of Thunderhead.

They camped on the North Carolina side of the meadow close to a small spring. They walked on up to Rocky Top that night for a look into the valley far below.

"On the way up we heard a tinkling sound around some big white rocks, and we were startled to see some moving white shapes," Herbert says. "We had disturbed a small flock of sheep that had bedded down for the night.

"We were to see them again in the morning, and Jim Francis was to make a picture at early dawn of some of the sheep still asleep on the ground."

LUMBER WAS A MAJOR MOUNTAIN PRODUCT

Post retraces ancestor's golden path in the Smokies

Eldorado: the "golden one" of Spanish-American folklore. A place of fabulous riches.

John Calvin Post II, about 60 years ago, took his son Jim (James C.) exploring along the headwaters of Hesse Creek. Their starting place was the old road, for many years the only road, from Cades cove across Rich Mountain into Tuckaleechee Cove.

Most of the upper Hesse Creek is now inside Great Smoky Mountains National Park. It's a swift, cascading stream until it reaches the gentler valley of West Miller Cove, where it flows into Little River.

The old road is open in the warmer months, for one-way travel only, from Cades Cove outbound. Where it fords Hesse Creek, over a concrete apron today, is where Jim and his father began their journey.

About a mile downstream they came to a pile of field stones that would have weighed about 50 tons, by Jim's recent estimate. "That," the father told the son, "was my grandfather's smelting furnace."

"To me it was nothing more than a pile of rock," Jim recalls, and I wondered why he had taken the trouble to take me down there."

But Jim now knows why his father "took the trouble." It is that some of us are drawn more to thinking about our parents and grandparents as time passes, and are more compelled to share what we learn with our own children.

Jim and Marian Post came back to Blount County to stay in the mid 1980s. He was retiring after a career as an engineer with the Aluminum Company of America. His last station, Marian there with him, was in Jakarta, Indonesia, for four years.

He has "taken the trouble" many times lately to further explore the Smoky Mountain paths of his parents, grandparents and great-grandparents.

The ancestor who left the pile of rocks was Dr. Calvin Post, Jim's great-grandfather. He was educated as a physician and metallurgist-geologist, but Jim says he is known to have enjoyed the latter far more than the practice of medicine.

Calvin was crippled in a riverboat explosion on his way to East Tennessee in the early 1840s. He recuperated at the Maryville home of William and Rebecca Wallace Thompson. He married their daughter Martha in 1846.

Jim says that soon after their marriage they lived for about a year in the Rich Gap wilderness, between Rich Mountain and Cades Cove Mountain, on the headwaters of Hesse Creek. Their first child, son John Calvin Post, (Jim's grandfather) was born there.

They named their forest paradise "Eldorado," implying that they looked upon it as a place where they would find gold. Calvin had leased the mineral rights from Dr. Isaac Anderson, founder of Maryville College.

Jim Post assumes that his great-grandfather had the resources to hire help for his mining venture. There are remains of projects, including shafts 30 feet deep, sides cleanly vertical, that are too big to have been done by one man alone.

In his papers there is a design for a reverberatory furnace, in which the heat was reflected from ceiling and walls onto the ore being smelted. The pile of rocks, to which Jim's father led him long ago, are the ruins of such a furnace. Its existence indicates that although Post didn't find gold, he might have found iron ore worth smelting for assay.

In Hesse Creek, the water preserving it these 140 years, are the remains of a hollowed-out hemlock log. Jim figures it was a flume to divert water to a wheel, to pump a bellows for a forced-air draft, to make charcoal in the furnace burn hotter.

Chestnut trees were plentiful in Eldorado, and Calvin probably manufactured and burned chestnut charcoal. Jim says we can scratch around and find charcoal ashes at the site today. We can see where Calvin pulled the dross (scum from molten ore) from his furnace.

Oak and poplar were Eldorado's gold

The Sparks family lived several generations in Cades Cove, farmed there, ranged cattle and other livestock on the crest of the Smokies above the cove, and in the 20th Century cut timber and sawmilled around its fringes.

All the Sparkses of whom we speak today are the children and grandchildren of Jane Potter and Nathan Sparks. Jane is recorded as owner of the first cast-iron cook-stove brought into Cades Cove. Cooking before then was done entirely in the fireplace.

A grandson, Howard Sparks, says Nathan and Jane at one time owned "most of the upper end of Cades Cove."

At least three of their sons, Tom, Sam and George, were involved in a logging contract between Rich Mountain and Cades Cove Mountain, on the headwaters of Hesse Creek, beginning in 1905. Howard was 13 years old that year and helped his father, George, drive a team of logging horses on some of the more gentle pulls, skidding logs to the saw mill site.

Bill Abbott and some of the Dunn brothers, all of the area of nearby Tuckaleechee Cove, had the main contract to cut that timber and saw it into lumber, Howard says. They were sawing it for Little River Lumber Co., which had moved into the valley four or five years previously and was already logging West Prong and Laurel Creek, and planning to push railroads up the other Smoky Mountain prongs of Little River.

A wood fired boiler sat just outside a shed which sheltered the circle saw and the steam engine. The shed was built to prevent sparks from the boiler flue from raining on the saw crew while they worked. A person could get burned painfully by those flying live embers, Howard says.

Too, the shed kept the rain, snow and dew from the steam engine and the woven belts that ran to the saw. The protecting roof made it

147

possible to leave the belts on at night. A wet belt would sag, stretch and "give" during sawing and cause shutdowns for adjustment, Howard says.

Wide-brim heavy felt hats worn by most of the men workers at the sawmill had more than cosmetic value. They were the safety hats of that time and place. They protected somewhat against falling sparks, and they would absorb at least some impact of a falling limb. They were not as protective as the safety helmet of today, but they were probably more comfortable to wear.

The Hesse Creek headwaters where the Abbott-Dunn sawmill was situated was called Eldorado (pronounced El'duh-ray-doe) in that day, Howard says. The original *El Dorado* was a mythical city of great wealth which the Spanish Conquerors hoped to find in South America.

The sawmill at Eldorado in the Smokies was bigger than most portable steam-powered sawmills of its time, Howard says. Its engine was not mounted on the chassis with the boiler as were some of the smaller rigs. Its engine was mounted on skids, and when it was set up to saw, steam was piped from the boiler on wheels, which was always parked as close as possible to the engine.

Saws of different diameter were put on the mill according to the size of the timber being sawed that day. The mill could saw about 10,000 board feet of lumber per day, which was big production for a portable rig, Howard says. Most of the timber harvested was oak, yellow poplar, white pine and yellow pine.

Howard says Eldorado, between Rich Mountain and Cades Cove Mountain, was in some of the roughest terrain ever logged by Little River Lumber Co. He believes that may have been the company's reason for having the timber cut and sawed on contract. The lumber was hauled in wagons to Little River Railroad's depot at Riverside, at the lower end of Tuckaleechee Cove.

In later years the company was able to lay rails to the headwaters of Hesse Creek, by a direct route that bypassed West Miller Cove and the lower stretch of Hesse Creek.

All that rough, scenic upper valley of Hesse Creek is now within the boundary of Great Smoky Mountains National Park.

Trails busy with transient lumberjacks

Tom Cooper and his son Bill had more company than they at first expected in their one-room cabin at Russell Field.

The logging companies were at their busiest in all the major valleys of the Smokies in those three years from 1914 to 1917. Many lumberjacks changed jobs often, and the fastest route to another job was sometimes to cross the Smokies on foot.

The Cooper cabin was beside the mountaintop trail that looked into the upper valleys of all the prongs of Little River on the Tennessee side, and to Twenty-Mile Creek, Eagle Creek, Hazel, Forney, Noland and Deep Creek on the North Carolina side.

There were timber-cutting ventures in most of those valleys in the years the Coopers were on the mountain.

The operation on Eagle Creek, and the sawmill at the old village of Fontana on the north bank of Little Tennessee River at the mouth of Eagle Creek, was the destination of most loggers crossing the mountain by way of Russell Field. Two of the upper branches of Eagle Creek have their beginning at the edge of Russell Field.

> *"You ought to go up there to Russell Field sometime. There's a knob out from it that looks down on Cades Cove, and I'd walk out there of a morning just to look. I'd be above the clouds with the sun shining, and it'd look like a solid ocean down there."*

"We fed a lot of people," Bill Cooper recalls. "They sometimes offered to pay, but my daddy wouldn't take any pay.

"One Sunday morning, I told my dad, let's go out on the knob. There were wild turkeys there and we were going to shoot just one, a young one just big enough for the two of us, so there wouldn't be any

149

waste. We did and cooked it and made gravy. We put it in that big dutch oven we had, about the size of a dishpan. We set it in the hot coals of the fireplace, and piled more coals on the lid. We took the lid off a time or two to turn the meat, but a dutch oven heats pretty much even from the top and bottom.

"After the turkey was cooked we made gravy, and it smelled so

Frame structure of the Fontana Hotel stood when the old village of Fontana was a logging camp before World War I. This Fontana was on the north side of Little Tennessee River near the mouth of Eagle Creek, directly to the south of Russell Field. Site is near TVA's Fontana Dam and is now covered by its waters. Tracks in foreground were of a spur line connecting at Bushnell, N.C., upriver with a Southern Railway main line.
—Picture from S. Winston Henry of Maryville.

good it made us all the hungrier. Then a bunch of them loggers came through and ate with us and I never got a bite of that turkey, and neither did my dad. There must have been a dozen men in that bunch.

"Most of those loggers would be wolf-hungry by the time they climbed the mountain from either direction. Those that knew we were up there usually planned on eating with us. That's been a long time but I don't remember that it bothered us much. There were plenty of wild turkeys and maybe we went out and shot another and started over. Most of the travelers didn't stay long. We didn't have room to keep them overnight. I think maybe a few times we kept some of them overnight, when the weather looked bad."

Bill continues:

"You ought to go up there to Russell Field sometime. There's a knob out from it that looks down on Cades Cove, and I'd walk out there of a morning just to look. I'd be above the clouds with the sun shining, and it'd look like a solid ocean down there.

"Rich Gap Mountain and Cades Cove Mountain on the other side looked like boats, only their tops showing above the clouds. The wind blows a lot at Russell Field. There's always the wind. I just loved it up there."

Southern depot at Bushnell, N. C., about 1912 or 1913. Southern Railway and its spur line downriver from Bushnell served the lumber ventures at North Carolina's flank with the Great Smoky Mountains. The backwaters of Fontana Lake now cover the site.

Russell laments passing of fire towers

All the fire lookout towers in the Great Smoky Mountains have been taken down. The solitary life of those who manned the towers is one less adventure for young people of the future.

Russell Edward Whitehead was one of the first fireguards after Great Smoky Mountains National Park was created in the 1920s. Now, at the age of 94, he has been retired from it longer than many of us have worked at our careers. He has been retired since the 1950s.

View of the lower end of Cades Cove from Rich Mountain fire tower was photographed on infrared film in 1951. There was still some row-cropping, mostly for corn to feed livestock, among the few families who still lived in the Cove and farmed tracts leased from the National Park Service. Infrared film "sees through" the Smoky Mountain haze and shows every topographic detail of the main high ridge of the Smokies beyond the Cove.

Russell once quit his fire lookout work for a job with the Aluminum Co. of America at Alcoa. Soon the Park Service coaxed him back. Nobody on their roster knew the mountains surrounding Cades Cove as well as he did. Nobody could watch from the Rich Mountain tower and define the location of a fire quite as accurately and quickly as he could.

Jeff Whitehead at Bunker Hill Fire Tower, Western Smokies, early '50s.

In Russell's working years a lookout spent about six months of the year in the tower and nearby cabin. They were the driest months when the woods were most prone to burn.

"When I'd first go up there in the spring I liked it fine," Russell says. "Then when I first went up in the fall it was good again – better than ever! In the fall I could stand up there and see every color of the rainbow, as far as I could look.

"But when the woods got dry in a long dry spell and farmers were burning trash around, it was aggravating then. Lots of farmers would get out after dark and burn trash. I'd have to stay in the tower until the fire was put out, and I'd already be dog-tired when the fire started– staying in that tower 12 to 15 hours a day."

Russell says all the towers in the Smokies had well-built cabins nearby. His quarters on Rich Mountain had a comfortable sleeping cot, a wood burner for a heating stove and an oil stove for cooking.

"It was a three-burner oil stove, and I could make coffee and fry meat at the same time," Russell says. "I didn't have much company, but when company came, they came in big gangs, maybe on Sunday. Then I wouldn't see anybody else except at a distance for the next week or two."

Fire lookout tower and cabin similar to the one in which Russell White-head spent several solitary years of his life. The cabin was comfortable, Russel said, but the sheet-iron cab atop the tower was not insulated against heat or cold. "I've put in many a cold, shivery hour up there freezing to death," he added.

Hannah Mountain, between Cades Cove and Little Tennessee River and between Abrams Creek and the main ridge of the Smokies, was one of his assignments in the very first years of the park. He was there before a tower was built and climbed a dead pine tree with strips nailed across its trunk to take a look around at intervals.

He lived in a tent and communicated by two-way radio. Finally a high tower and cabin quarters were built there, on Bunker Hill, but that was after Russell had moved on to Rich Mountain.

Russell was divorced more than 50 years ago from his only wife, and he says he has been somewhat of a loner since, both in seasons at the fire towers and away from them. In off-seasons he boarded with friends in Cades Cove and Happy Valley. He is in touch with his two surviving children, daughter Gaynelle Loos of Oxnard, Calif., and son Cleo Whitehead of Norwalk, Calif. Cleo traveled here to visit him recently.

These last few years he has dwelt at Chilhowee Nursing Center on Montvale Station Road at Maryville. He has exceptional health for his almost 94 years. He prefers a room to himself, or at least a room-mate who listens neither to radio nor television. "I read a lot," Russell says. Young people come to him these days to ask his help in school projects. They come to ask about life in Cades Cove before Great Smoky Mountains National Park was created. He willingly tells them about his youth as

> *"In the fall I could stand up there and see every color of the rainbow, just as far as I could look. But when the woods got dry in a long dry spell and farmers were burning trash around, it was aggravating then."*
> *— Russell Whitehead*

one of 11 children of Taylor Whitehead and Mary Jane Gregory. He tells them his boyhood was austere by the standards of today's children, but he lets them know he values the gentle ways his parents taught him.

Russell very much enjoys telling of his experience herding cattle on Gregory Bald. He recalls his dislike of the "rough life" in the log-ging camps of nearby Little River. "I wasn't built for the kind of men that occupied them camps," he says. "I've tried them a few days at a time, but I never could be satisfied in them."

Sometimes he will tell a young audience of the darker side of the Cades Cove history he knows, to let them know it was not all idyllic. Many of his younger visitors are impressed by his age. Maybe it was what he ate, he tells them – bear lettuce, poke greens, ramps and wild mustard, and spring water to drink. Russell smiles when he says it, because he knows it's an answer that's far too simple.

One of his satisfactions was the case of a young girl who came with pencil and tablet and made notes as he told her his family sur-vived the Depression of the 1930s. "She turned it in for a school paper, and then she came back and told me she made an A on it. I was proud of that," Russell says.

Gnat smoke

Are gnats, the tiny no-see-ums, more plentiful around Great Smoky Mountains National Park now than they were before the park was created? We hear arguments that they are more abundant now than formerly. The usual explanation is that the old-timers kept the compost forest floor, the habitat of gnats, burned off.

But some believe gnats are no more numerous or pestiferous now than they were 50 years ago. Among them are Dulcie and Millard McCaulley, Old Walland Highway, Maryville, and George W. Myers, Berry Road, Knox County. All were born and grew up in the Smokies.

George and Millard say they have plowed many a day in Cades Cove, their birthplace, with a piece of burning, smoldering rag tied to the plowbeam, so the smoke would help keep the gnats away.

"They'd eat your ears off while you plowed if you didn't do something like that," says George.

Mrs. McCaulley, born an Abbott, remembers the metal bucket with rags smoldering in it that they kept in the yard when they sat out there on summer evenings.

There were other ways to build a "gnat smoke." One was to build a small wood fire and so cover it with wood chips that it would be mostly smoke and little or no flame.

As in other valleys around the Smokies, the Cades Cove gnats were locally known as "Domineckers," Millard says. Their nickname came, of course, from the big, aggressive Dominecker chickens which many families kept in those days.

There's a cairn of small stones in the woods above the Cades Cove Missionary Baptist Church, which stands at the junction of the new Loop Road and the old road across Rich Mountain. It would be hard to guess the reason for it if we didn't have somebody tell us.

Millard's father, John McCaulley, said they were carried there one at a time by people who went to that spot to pray, usually before church took up on Sunday morning. It got to be a custom to take a rock along and make the pile grow.

June10, 1982

ABOUT BELLS IN THE MOUNTAINS 9

Tinkling bells were mountain radar

The Great Smoky Mountains had been set aside as a national park, and early in 1934 the livestock herders were allowed "just one more summer" to range the mile-high meadows above Cades Cove.

Ernest Tipton, now of Townsend, made a camping trip to Thunderhead Mountain in 1934, and he remembers the melancholy of the herders there, that this would be the final season of a livelihood that had been so adventurous.

There was no other local way of earning a living that gave as much personal freedom. There were few places anywhere that offered such pleasant daily vistas of sunrise and sunset, of valleys and other mountain ranges to every horizon.

Herman Hodge and Sam Tipton spent the final summer on and around Gregory Bald, about a mile high and a steep walk of about seven miles from the lower, or western end of Cades Cove. Herman's oldest of seven children, his son Raymond, lived on the mountain with them, in a two-room cabin on the Tennessee side of the line, close to the gant lot at Moore Spring.

"I was 11 years old, not old enough or big enough to help much with the cattle. School was out in May, and I stayed up there until cattle gathering time about Labor Day. All of us came home then," Raymond says.

Herman and Sam looked after several hundred head of cattle, mostly other people's livestock, the final season. In summers long ago there had been far bigger herds on the same mountain, as many as 800 head pastured in the grassy, open, sunlit forests at the shoulder of the bald.

There were no fences around the high pastures, but a lone herdsman sometimes kept watch over all the cattle consigned to him. He did it with the help of cattle salt and cowbells.

Block salt was awkward to carry so the cattle salt brought to the bald range was loose salt in cloth sacks hauled up the mountain on the backs of mules or horses.

Raymond Hodge, whose parents, Betty Tipton and Herman Hodge, were both from Cades Cove, holds some of the livestock bells his father collected from friends and along mountain cattle trails beginning in 1913. Hole in one bell may have been from somebody's poor marksmanship at cattle slaughter time.

The herder on his daily rounds of all the grassy patches, a few cattle at this one and maybe a dozen or more at the next one, would take with him as much salt as he could handle walking.

Sometimes he carried a small axe to chop a flat, smooth place in a fallen log. He'd create a "lick" there, from which the salt would not escape readily when it rained. The cattle savored the salt, and ordinarily wouldn't stray from a place where it was available.

To make it possible to find cattle and sheep and hogs from day to day in those countless acres of mountain wilderness, the animals were belled. There were big bells, often home-made, for cattle, and smaller, high-pitched bells for sheep and hogs. Some of the farmers who entrusted their cattle to Herman and Sam

158

for the summer owned as few as a half-dozen, and some owned several dozen. Each owner hung a bell around the neck of one or more cows in his herd.

These were older animals that were leaders of the rest of the herd. The more cattle an owner took to the mountain, the more bells there would be among them.

Each bell had a voice of its own, and the herders would learn to know the voices of the bells. They could tell, for instance, by the sound of a bell whether it was Dave Hill's cattle grazing nearby, although they might be hidden from view by the forest or by darkness.

Before his death in 1967, Herman Hodge became an authority on the history and use of Smoky Mountain livestock bells. Each bell had a *voice* of its own, and when a herder heard a certain bell he could identify it, and thus know whose cattle were grazing in the area from which the sound came.

Herman began collecting livestock bells when he was 13 years old and the Rev. John W. Oliver of Cades Cove gave him a calf bell, Raymond says. Through the years he found more along the trails from Cades Cove to the several nearby bald ranges. Usually they were bells that had fallen because the leather neck straps had worn through. Eventually he had a collection of more than 150 bells, many of them identified as to had originally owned it. Actually they're not all cowbells. Some were used for sheep, hogs, horses, and even turkeys.

At one time there was a bell-ringing contest with a panel of judges to decide which bell had the best "voice." The winner was a cowbell with a low, rich tinkle and a story behind it. In 1865, at close of the Civil War, George Shields decided he would leave Cades Cove and move his family and possessions to Oklahoma Territory, and this bell was one of the things taken along, But George didn't like Oklahoma and soon moved back to Cades Cove. The bell came back with him.

There was a bell with a bullet hole in it and this one had belonged to Jim Russell. The bullet hole was the result of somebody's poor marksmanship at cattle-slaughter time. The bullet went through the bell but missed the steer.

Cowbells and turkey bells

We traveled toward Walland to visit Herman Hodge in his natural habitat on Rocky Branch. It's Herman who has the big collection of cowbells. Actually they're not all cowbells. Some were used to bell sheep, and hogs, and horses, and even turkeys.

Herman's collection now numbers 150 bells and he hasn't quit looking. He has a bell which once belonged to Becky Cable, whose old home in Cades Cove is preserved as part of an exhibit of pioneer life.

He has a bell which went to Oklahoma and back with George Shields. George went west by wagon, but yearned for his old home in Cades Cove so much he returned. That old bell got such a workout, hung from the neck of an ox, tinkling all the way to Oklahoma and back and for years afterward, that it was worn through in places when Herman first acquired it. He has since brazed the worn places.

Cowbell has hole from rifle ball.

One of the bells has a hole in it, which was put there by a good-sized rifle bullet, probably a ball from a muzzle loader.

Each bell is marked as to who owned it, if Herman knows who owned it. Some were found on the high balds of the Smokies, where area residents grazed their cattle and sheep in summer before the mountains became a National Park.

Herman worked at herding cattle up there in the summer, and has a good guess as to who owned some of the unidentified bells. But he tags only those whose owners he is certain of.

Rena Ledbetter's bell rescued bees

Manuel and Rena Shields Ledbetter lived in a house near what is now the riding horse stables across from Cades Cove campground. Some of the roses Rena planted still bloom, among the pines that have grown there in the more than half-century since.

The Ledbetters farmed, and in the spring and summer most of the

Manuel "Man" Ledbetter and wife Rena Shields

family would be in the fields working most days, with only Rena at the house. She had a big cowbell she rang to call all of them to the house for the noon meal, called dinner in that time and place.

She also rang the bell to call them all in when the bees swarmed, and for that reason she called it "my bee bell."

One of her six surviving children, Maynard Ledbetter, a resident of Frogtown Road near Townsend for most of the 53 years since he and his wife Mary moved out of Cades Cove, says a bee swarm in May or June was a big event, one that meant more honey in the crock for the winter ahead.

"That's the way the bees multiplied," Maynard says. "There'd be a swarm of bees follow a new queen out of an old hive, and settle on a tree limb. We'd put the swarm in a new bee gum, and we'd have one more hive to gather honey for us."

Bees that swarmed in May or June still had a long season of cloverbloom and other flowers ahead for storing a surplus of honey in their new home. Bees that swarmed later than June would be hard pushed to make enough for their own winter sustenance.

A swarm of bees in May is worth a ton of hay.
A swarm of bees in June is worth a silver spoon.
A swarm of bees in July is not worth a fly.

Maynard remembers when almost everybody in his little Smoky Mountain world called a beehive a bee gum. That was because they were made, a long time back, from short sections of hollow log of the black gum tree.

View deep into a log beehive shows both cross-sticks, to which the bees hung their honeycomb, piling it above and below. Roof of the hive, to protect it from skunks, was boards weighted with rocks.

"Our people hunted hollow trees in the mountains. They'd cut them into blocks of two or three or four feet long. They'd clean them out good, and maybe hollow them out more to where there'd be more room inside," Maynard says.

"They wouldn't always be gum trees. They might be basswood, and the ironwood tree made a good round bee gum. But whatever kind of tree it was, they still called it a bee gum.

"They'd put two cross-sticks through the lower part of the hollow, about a third of the way from the bottom. The bees would form their honeycombs on the cross-sticks, and they'd keep building higher into the hive."

"When my people got ready to rob a bee gum, they'd say let's get the honey down to the cross-sticks.

"They took out the honey with a crooked butcher knife, a long knife with a bent blade. What honey was below the cross-sticks, they'd leave for the bees to feed on.

"Most everybody in Cades Cove kept a few stands of bees in those days. That's the way the families got most of their sweetening."

As soon as sawed lumber became plentiful in the Cove, early in the century, Manuel "Man" Ledbetter began making beehives the way we now picture them – neat, uniform, box-shaped, and painted white.

Son Maynard keeps bees today, at several foot-of-mountain locations around Townsend. His hives now are all boxes.

"I haven't had a hollow log beehive in years, but I still call them *bee-gums,*" Maynard says. "And like as not I always will."

An Era Comes to an End

10

Lifelong roots difficult to transplant

The John W. Oliver farm of nearly 400 acres was in the lower end of Cades Cove on the north side of Abrams Creek. There was one farm between the Olivers and the gorge through which Abrams Creek leaves the Cove. Wayne Oliver says his parents did not oppose creation of Great Smoky Mountains National Park in the late 1920s and early 1930s. He says they did, however, want very much to remain in Cades Cove.

"The roots of a lifetime run very deep," Wayne says. "My father was born and raised there. His parents before him lived their lives in Cades Cove."

Judge Oliver recalls for us some of his father's legal steps in the first four years of the 1930s, first to try to keep his land, and then his successful lawsuit to be paid more money than the state first offered.

"When early efforts were being made to establish a Great Smoky Mountains National Park, the idea was for the state of Tennessee to acquire the needed land on its side, and for North Carolina to acquire the land within its borders.

"The first negotiators, people seeking to acquire the land, came into Cades Cove and told the people that they would not be disturbed if the park should be established, and would be permitted to stay there.

"As it turned out, the people were not permitted to stay in the Cove after their land was acquired, with three or four exceptions.

The misrepresentation annoyed a lot of the people, including my father.

"In the beginning his counsel, R. R. Kramer, a great man and a great lawyer, took the position that the State of Tennessee could not constitutionally exercise its power of eminent domain for the benefit of another sovereign, to wit, the United States.

"In the trial court that position was sustained by Judge Pat Quinn, and of course the state appealed to the Supreme Court of Tennessee.

"And that court disagreed with Judge Quinn. It held that one

Cades Cove Consolidated School housed eight elementary grades and looked like this after the second floor was removed. The second floor had been an auditorium with a basketball court, a library room and a classroom. Entire downstairs was classrooms. Wayne Oliver attended this school before he became a student at Professor Billy Joe Henry's private school in Maryville.

sovereign, to wit the State of Tennessee, was constitutionally authorized to exercise its power of eminent domain to acquire land to be turned over to the United States in fee simple, for the establishment of a national park."

"From then on the question was to decide the market value of the land my father owned in Cades Cove.

"In condemnation cases, the condemner, whether it be the state or any subdivision thereof, seeking to acquire property for public purposes by eminent domain, is to establish a jury of view composed of five qualified people whose duty is to go upon the property and examine it, and hear any proof offered by the state or by the landowners or both, and then determine the fair cash market value of the property in question.

"That is all that any government is required to pay for property being acquired for public use. The fair cash market value is all that any landowner is entitled to claim.

"In my father's case the jury of view, after going through all that procedure, fixed the value of his property at $10,650. He appealed from that award to the Circuit Court, where the case was tried by a jury of 12 citizens. In that trial, the jury awarded my parents $16,500. I believe that's the figure.

"That effectively was the end of the litigation about my father's property in Cades Cove. It had been to the Tennessee Supreme Court three times before it was resolved."

Wayne says his parents left the Cove in 1937, the year the park took control of the land and the year of greatest native exodus. The Olivers built a new home in Mitchell Hollow at Townsend.

Nancy Ann died there in 1948 at the age of 70, and John W. died there in 1966 at the age of 88. Both are buried in the Primitive Baptist Church cemetery in Cades Cove.

Sleep free in the 'stranger bed'

George Tipton and wife Tuckaleechee (Aunt Tuck) had the last of their 12 children early in the century, while the family lived on Rowans Creek at the southeast corner of Cades Cove. The Tiptons lived beside the trail from the cove up the creek to Russell Field. The same trail led across the mountain into the valley of Eagle Creek on the North Carolina side.

There were days when several strangers would pass, walking to or from logging jobs then plentiful in valleys on both sides of the Smokies. There were times when a traveler would ask for a bed for the night and something to eat.

Ella Tipton Abbott was born in 1899 and is one of four surviving children of the Tiptons. Here is what she remembers of sheltering wayfarers, most of them unknown to the family.

"There was a bed that none of our family ever slept in. It was saved for company and we called it the *stranger bed.* If somebody came by, even at night, my daddy wouldn't turn them away. We fed them, too, supper and breakfast. And nobody ever paid for it that I can remember.

"It must have been hard on mother to prepare the food, but she had to cook so much for so many children that there was usually enough for one more.

"One thing I remember about breakfast – whoever was there – Grandfather Martin Tipton lived with us the last 10 years of his life and mother served him first.

"We bought bean coffee. Mother ground it fresh every morning in a little coffee mill that hung on the wall. We knew it was breakfast time when we heard that little mill grinding Then when everybody was seated at the table, she'd pour Grandpa Tipton's coffee first.

"Of course not all us children were at home at the same time. Some of the older ones had married and moved away when the last two were born. But there was always a crowd at the table."

Ella says that only the older children drank coffee regularly. "Sometimes mother would pour a little, just a taste of it, in the milk of some of us younger ones," she says.

George Tipton's main calling at the turn of the century was looking after other people's cattle on and around Gregory Bald in the warm months, beginning the first of May and ending early in September, on Labor Day.

The home on Rowans Creek was at the opposite end of Cades Cove from the trail to Gregory Bald. When Tipton left home in the spring he'd be gone most of the summer, with only a seldom visit to his family when an older son or relative *spelled* him off on the mountain.

Mack and John Hitch and some of the Davises were among the main families who brought their cattle to George to be tended for the season. Ella says they paid him an agreed price per animal for the whole summer, and she believes it was a dollar or $1.25 a head.

"I'm not sure but I believe that's the way he paid for our farm on Rowans Creek, with his money from herding cattle," Ella says. Meanwhile, the task of raising food for the family, and of laying some of it away for the winter ahead, went to Margaret Tuckaleechee Burchfield Tipton and her older children. Ella's memory is that they ate reasonably well in all seasons.

Most of the discipline of the children was self-discipline, she says. "I saw two of my middle brothers in a fistfight only one time.

My mother and daddy didn't live in a fuss. They didn't whip and beat on the children. I never did hear them quarrel.

"Of course I was only 12 years old when my mother died," Ella says.

Wilderness swallows Aunt Tuck's farm

Chance of a heavy snowfall was thought to be past by late April, even at higher levels of the Great Smoky Mountains.

So it was about that time of year that George Tipton would go to Gregory Bald, to the gant lot corral at Moore Spring, to begin receiving the several hundred head of cattle that he would tend for the next several months.

George's wife Tuckaleechee (Aunt Tuck) and those of their 12 children born up to that time knew it would be at least weeks, and

Asa Sparks' tractor was preparing a Cades Cove field for planting corn in 1949. Beyond the tractor is the long hollow of Rowans Creek descending from Thunderhead Mountain at distant center. George and Margaret Tuckaleechee Tipton and their 12 children lived in the lower valley of Rowans Creek, but above the Cades Cove plain. The National Park Service quit leasing cove land for growing corn and other row crops in the 1970s and quit renewing livestock grazing permits beyond the end of the 20th Century.

maybe months, before they would see him again.

All the older children, boys and girls, meanwhile were in one of the family's busy seasons at the home on Rowans Creek, close to where the park service's Cades Cove campground now stands.

Time to go to the mountain with the cattle was also time to plant corn and beans in the lowland, and maybe to hoe the first potato sprouts showing above ground.

The wild woods had already given their first edible greens of spring-time, lamb's tongue, crow's foot, bear lettuce and pokeweed, and ramps from high in the hollow.

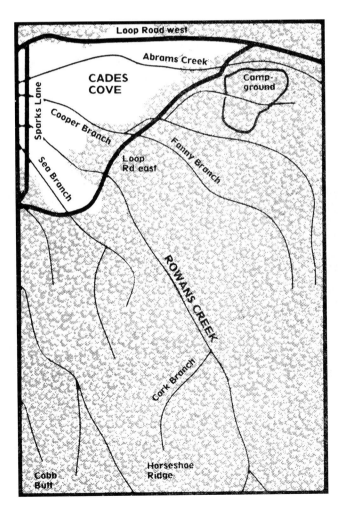

Map of Cades Cove shows Rowans Creek flowing toward its junction with Abrams Creek from the main ridge of the Smokies. The Loop Road crosses Rowans Creek by bridge a short distance from Cades Cove Campground.

It had been most of a winter since the family had tasted anything fresh and green, and Ella Tipton Abbott says she and her brothers and sisters savored the wild *salit*, cooked like today's garden greens or *killed* with hot bacon grease and vinegar.

"My mother knew all the green things and when and where to find them," Ella says. Ella was born in 1899 and says her memory goes back rather clearly to when she was six years old – in 1905.

"My mother had just a few glass canning jars then. She'd save the jars to can blackberries – things we couldn't save by drying. She'd have us children out picking wild gooseberries, and we'd dry them on muslin sheets in the sun. (A dried gooseberry would look something like a currant, or small raisin.)

Betty Tipton Seaton and daughter Eugenia Spencer visit the chimney ruins of what the family called the *fire room* of their Cades Cove grandparents' place on Rowans Creek. Both women are nurses, Seaton at Blount Memorial Hospital and Spencer at University of Tennessee Hospital.
Photo by nurse Gretchen Kirkland.

"We dried all the beans we saved for winter. First we'd tear away the string that gives string beans their name. Then mother would set us children down and give each a needle and thread. We'd thread the beans until we had a string a yard or two long. We'd tie it in a loop and hang them behind the stove to dry. They'd get shuck-dry and we'd call them *leather breeches*," Ella says.

When they were needed for a meal, they were taken from the string and parboiled briefly. That water was discarded and the beans were then cooked fully in new water, usually with a piece of pork.

The family also preserved green beans each year by pickling them in salt in a crock. Pickled beans thus were made about the same way cabbage was made into sauerkraut. Beans raised for soup beans were allowed to dry on the vine in the garden, and were shelled and saved in cloth sacks.

Potatoes, turnips and cabbage in the head were saved in a straw-lined hole under a mound of earth. "We'd keep cabbage the whole winter that way – turn the roots up and the head down, put straw on and throw dirt over. When we dug it out of there it'd be just as crisp and tender!" Ella says.

Aunt Tuck made jelly and apple butter for her family long before she had glass jars and paraffin for seal. When blackberries were ripe, she'd make a run of jelly from sugar and juice only. "Two measures of juice to one measure of sugar," Ella says. She had no fruit pectin.

The jelly was kept in a covered crock in the cold water of the springhouse. Enough was taken from the crock for each meal. Apple butter was stored in the same manner. Refined sugar was scarce and apple butter was cooked with molasses or honey as the sweetener.

The Tiptons also saved large quantities of peeled and quartered apples by drying them in the sun. The dried fruit would be cooked into applesauce that winter, and some of the applesauce went into the making of stack cakes. It was a cake of several thin layers, with applesauce at every layer.

George and Tuckaleechee Tipton had grapevines and an apple orchard at the home on Rowans Creek. But Ella says that when she walked back in there three years ago, "I saw nothing living of what my father had planted. The last big apple tree had fallen. It looked like it had been down for years. The woods had overrun all our old fields. The spring was still there, and the water was so clear somebody must have cleaned it out just ahead of us.

"The rock my father put beside it was there, too. My mother would stand on that rock to dip water from the spring, and I stood a long time and thought about my mother."

Ella Abbott says her family moved out of Cades Cove in 1932 when their property was sold to be included in Great Smoky Mountains National Park.

They had a sprout of a Sour John apple tree they brought out of the park with them and planted at their new home near Maryville.

Now the sprout is a tree, and Mrs. Abbott makes applesauce and bright red apple jelly from its fruit each fall.

Betty Tipton Seaton at the spring her grandparents used for a water supply.

"Most of the Sour Johns are dead and have been replaced with a fancier-looking apple, but in no wise better," Ella says.

Unpublished

Will the last to leave please blow out the light?

Lois and Kermit Caughron may be the very last family to have lived most of their lives and all of their married years in Cades Cove. Kermit lived outside the Cove only for several years of school in the 1920s and a few weeks in a nursing home before his death in April of 1999 at the age of 87. Lois left the Cove in 1936 when she was 12 years old and her parents, Will Shuler and Laura Anthony, vacated

Kermit Caughron hoes a row of onions in his Cades Cove garden.

their land to the new national park then being assembled in the Smokies. Lois returned in 1942 after marrying Kermit, who had begun what was to be a lifelong career of leasing park land as pasture for his beef cattle.

Thus the Caughrons were to live in their native Smoky Mountain valley from 1942 until close to the end of the 20th Century. They raised two daughters and two sons there with the weathered, well ventilated old Peter Cable house as their

175

first habitat. Lois also calls it the Dan Lawson house because she believes that Dan, who was Peter's son-in-law, built it. The Caughrons put linoleum down to try to shut out some of the draft and make up for the lack of underpinning, but a strong breeze under the floor would still lift the linoleum.

Kermit salvaged lumber from a dismantled school to begin building a new house, a more weatherproof dwelling to the rear of the Dan Lawson place and farther from the Loop Road, at the edge of the woods and at the foot of the main ridge of the Smokies, the mountain that is the south wall of Cades Cove. The house was completed in the early 1950s and friends who visited were impressed by its rustic coziness.

It was not, however, the kind of *cozy* Lois was looking for. Without electricity she would have neither air conditioning nor window fans. Without an electric stove or water heater she would be cooking, canning, and heating water on a wood-burning kitchen range with firewood to carry in and ashes to carry out. Heating water for several washes over several hours left the house stifling hot in the warm months, and wash day with infant children coming along could be twice a week or more often.

The water system was a gravity feed from a spring reservoir on the hill and the pipe that brought the water into the house later became a summertime water heater. Black plastic pipe – 400 feet of it laid back and forth on the slope where it would be in direct sunlight – heated the water while carrying it to the house. On a sunny day it would heat enough for three washes with some left for personal bathing, all without the help of the kitchen stove.

A portable generator to supply electricity for a new washing machine was the next home improvement step. The old washer got its power directly from a gasoline engine mounted under it – an engine that Lois had difficulty starting.

The generator was seldom used except to run the washing machine. The family never did have television in Cades Cove. Their kerosene refrigerator was replaced in time with one that burned butane, but neither was as convenient as the electrical wonder waiting for when they'd move out of the Cove. For pressing clothes they tried a gasoline iron, but it soon stayed on the shelf in deference to an old-style flatiron heated on the back of the wood-burner in the kitchen.

Lois says Kermit enjoyed playing the pioneer, doing things the hard way, the old way, living the way his parents and grandparents had lived, and that he tried to make his way acceptable to her and their children by taking on more than his share of the more onerous chores, although there was seldom anything in the line of food preparation that she was left completely out of.

Lois and Kermit in their kale patch.

Because he didn't like margarine and considered cow butter a necessity, he kept one milk cow apart from the big herds of beef cattle and reserved for himself the job of milking twice a day. Lois saved the cream until it clabbered and churned it to butter in her hand-cranked churn. The routine lasted about 55 years of the 57 years they were married.

The kitchen range and a fireplace in the living room heated the house through their early married years, with Kermit sawing and splitting most of the firewood and kindling. Many times after supper he would announce he was going out to cut firewood. He was handy with an ax and the pile would grow fast, and when he went to bed he would fall asleep almost immediately. After they had been married maybe 25 years, Lois doesn't remember exactly when it was, they bought a factory-made wood-burning heater for the living room. Except that Lois had to refill it with wood every two hours every night, every day, the new stove heated the house much better than the fireplace did. But Lois says it was a cold house whatever they tried to heat it with.

It was Kermit who won the attention of newspaper and television people through the years. A new seasonal ranger had seen the stories, without mention of Lois, and came to the Cove thinking Kermit lived alone. When he saw Lois in the yard he warned Kermit, "I believe you may have a prowler back there."

A friend of the Caughrons was wondering why as leaseholders they had chosen to move into the Dan Lawson place when there were other places more comfortable and with a better view of the valley and surrounding mountains. Lois says it was Kermit's choice to live at the Lawson place, probably because there were already mature fruit trees on the plot and because he had planted more trees. When the fruit ripened there would be a race with the bears to harvest it.

The Caughrons planted gardens every summer they lived in the Cove, often with tourist cameras pointed at them as they worked. Kermit's hoe had been the hoe used by his mother, Delia Myers Caughron, and he liked to lift and show it to dramatize how worn it was. Beans, corn, tomatoes, okra, potatoes, greens, turnips, and cucumbers were planted every year, sometimes with seed saved from last summer's crop. Kermit liked the short white cucumber from seeds handed down by his mother – thought it was the only cucumber worth having.

Their daughter Ruth Caughron Davis says: "Dad grew everything. The only groceries we had to buy were lard, baking powder, flour, salt, sugar and coffee. We kept potatoes buried in straw. We canned green beans, peaches, apples, pickles, greens. We'd buy pinto beans by the 100-pound sack. We had peaches, apples, cherries, blueberries, strawberries growing there close to the house. We moved nearly

400 quart jars of canned food when our mother moved out of the Cove in 1999."

Kermit's honor system for roadside sales of honey was in the news and became a bigger story when he set a trap for people who didn't pay for the honey they took. He built a blind in which he would hide at peak traffic times and pop up to remind defaulters: no money, no honey.

He caught very few offenders, but for other reasons began easing out of the honey business. It may have been Lois, more reserved than her cowboy husband, who reminded him that he was more than a little bit successful in his cattle ranging enterprise.

There were signs, too, that his success had made him more dignified, although there would be lapses, as on the evening he wore a new pair of gallus overalls to a grandson's otherwise white-tie wedding ceremony.

Lois did not regret the closing of the honey stand. She was allergic to bees, afraid of them, and never did try to learn much about them. She was afraid of snakes, too, and rather than go to the woodshed after seeing a copperhead there, she had let the fire in the cookstove die a time or so.

Early in 1998, their son Roy had city water connected to property where Kermit had lived during his only years out of Cades Cove. Roy asked his Dad to move out to this place where they could have electricity and Lois could better care for him.

Was Kermit ready to move?

"No, Lois. You can go. You move on out there if you want to. I'll stay here in the Cove. I was born here, you know. My mother and daddy lived here. I'll stay here, Lois. I'll be fine. I've been here more than 85 years. That's right, isn't it? Eighty-five years."

Lois couldn't consider moving out of the Cove and leaving Kermit behind. He couldn't take his prescribed medicine without someone to help him. He couldn't feed himself for long without help. So, she would stay with Kermit as she had stayed by him for more than 55 years.

Kermit's health had been declining and he would have to go to the hospital for treatment every month or so. After one of these hospital stays, the doctor released him with the condition that he not return to the Cades Cove house without a constant heat source and so far from the hospital. This time he didn't balk. Lois went to the nursing home and sat with him every day while Roy continued preparing the new home to try to make them both more comfortable.

But that was not to happen for Kermit Caughron. He died at Blount Memorial Hospital on April 5, 1999.

Lois has since moved into the new home north of Crooked Creek and Chilhowee Mountain, a home with a thermostat that calls up warm or cool temperatures almost in an instant. There are comforts and gadgets they never enjoyed in the Cove: electric freezer, refrigerator, electric clothes dryer, electric lights with no wicks to be trimmed; hot and cold water day and night, big screen television, and a view of Chilhowee Mountain from a recliner in the living room, in the direction of Cades Cove and the Smokies beyond.

And if the electric lights should fail, one of the oil lamps they carried room to room in Cades Cove is kept where it can be found in a hurry.

>*Note:* *The name is spelled Caughron but several genera-*
>*tions of the family in and around the Great Smoky Mountains*
>*have been pronouncing it Cau-HORN. Also, some of the*
>*Caughrons are changing the spelling to Caughorn. Roy*
>*Caughron, who grew up pronouncing it CauHORN, believes*
>*his pronunciation to be as old as the name itself. He is aware*
>*of a movement to return to what others are saying is the way*
>*it was pronounced by his Scots-Irish ancestors. That would*
>*be something like CARrun, accent on the first syllable.*
>   *—VW*

Vic Weals
1918-2001

EPILOGUE

(The last piece Vic Weals wrote)

John and Dora White supplied a bucket and invited me to help myself to the big juicy blackberries ripening along Crooked Creek behind their Blount County home. That was probably in July of 1947, less than two years after I was discharged from the wartime Army and about a year after I left a job as shipping clerk in a West Virginia steel mill to move to East Tennessee. It was a month after I had begun work with *The Journal,* Knoxville's morning daily and Sunday newspaper, in a career I would continue fitfully for another 39 years. Too, in 1947, I was a student at the University of Tennessee, living in a house trailer on The Hill through 1948.

John White appeared to enjoy reciting the lore of Crooked Creek, Chilhowee Mountain and the Great Smoky Mountains as much as I enjoyed listening. He and Dora lived on the historic Blockhouse Road in 1947. Dora had since passed away but John still lived there, 99 years old, when I visited in 2001 in the final weeks of putting this book together. If he made it to Dec. 23, 2001, he would be 100 years old, he said. It was John who briefed me on that valley north and west of Chilhowee Mountain being the footpath expressway of the Little Tennessee River tribes to the French Broad Valley and beyond. Probably they had walked through what is now his property and may have feasted on the blackberries. It was from John and his neighbors that I first heard that nearby Wilkinson Pike from Maryville to Greasy Cove and up Chilhowee Mountain through Butterfly Gap had been the route of cattle drovers taking their herds to spring pasture in the Smokies.

John himself raised beef cattle from his family's brood stock, their own cows and bulls. The Whites cleared 40 acres of knob land south of Blockhouse Road and sowed it to grass for permanent pasture close to home. There was a barn on the knob tract big enough to shelter the herd through cold, wet weather. John's father, Alse White, was a cattle trader who marked his stock the Western way, by scorching his brand, the letter 'A', into the animal's flank. John can't remember anyone who branded any other way.

Microfilm and memories
let Vic Weals go on forever

Now I have made my last contribution to the Knoxville Journal. I have written it on my own word processor at home, and will plug it into the telephone to deliver it to the newspaper.

Helen and I are meanwhile left with loads of column artifacts. There are hundreds of negatives and pictures, some historical, many never in the paper. There are volumes of clippings bound chronologically and dating from 1951. There are hundreds of audio tapes of people remembering their lives earlier in the century, or in the century before.

Because it has been a joint effort with the families involved, we promise not to throw away any of it. My sister, Mary Burriss, made a good start toward indexing it sometime ago, and now maybe we'll have time to finish organizing it.

My family, my children and four grandchildren, will help sometime to decide what to do with it, excepting the original telegrams and other papers from the Scopes Evolution Trial. Those are promised to John Dobson of the UT Special Collections Library.

Most of what we have will probably go to the McClung Historical Collection, which has kept a clipping file under my name since 1980, and whose staff has been kind to me in many helpful ways. We also admire the archival work done by Great Smoky Mountains National Park, and may contribute to it.

The vain thought arises that everything I have written for the newspaper, since joining it for the first time in 1947, is preserved in the Journal microfilm files of several libraries, and that as long as the microfilm survives, there will be a Vic Weals column in the Knoxville Journal. The same thought allows me to regret on this last day, that I wrote so much that was trivial a few years back.

There are other things to be said about my newspaper years, but if I say them it will be in another forum. Maybe I'll also talk about my time as a student, soldier, Great Lakes sailor, steel mill worker, and 10 busy years as a television network news stringer (cameraman and reporter, on demand).

Our friendships with the people who have helped record some of the oral history of East Tennessee have been especially satisfying. Let's stay in touch.

This is the last column Vic Weals wrote for the Knoxville Journal. His books are now on sale at the Great Smoky Mountains Visitors Center and at East Tennessee area bookstores. The mail address is Olden Press, 4403 Cypress Drive, Knoxville, Tennessee 37920.

– Editor